ERIK ROUTLEY was born, to the day, four hundred years after Martin Luther nailed up his 95 theses! Now a Congregational minister, he has held various pastoral charges and served as tutor at Mansfield College, Oxford. He is a regular contributor to the *British Weekly* and has been editor of the British Hymn Society for the last ten years. In 1955 he was Old St. Andrew's Memorial Lecturer at Victoria University, Toronto. He holds the degrees of B.D., M.A., and Ph.D. from Oxford University.

*The Wisdom
of the Fathers*

The Wisdom
of the Fathers

by

ERIK ROUTLEY

Philadelphia

THE WESTMINSTER PRESS

*First published in Great Britain in 1957
by the S.C.M. Press, Ltd., London*

Library of Congress Catalog Card No.: 57-9568

91324466

*Typeset in Great Britain
Printed in the United States of America*

To the
FELLOWSHIP OF YOUNG
CONGREGATIONALISTS
of Northumberland and Durham, and to
Ralph Bell of Otterburn Hall, I gratefully
dedicate these pages, because Ralph is
the most improbable theologian I know,
and one of the most effective, and
because the Fellowship is the best
audience I have ever encountered in
discussion of the best subjects

CONTENTS

PREFACE

I N a book that I have consulted in preparing the following chapters, C. S. Lewis wrote of the 'strange idea that in every subject the ancient books should be read only by the professionals, and that the amateur should content himself with the modern books'. He wrote that in the Introduction to a new translation of the *De Incarnatione* of Athanasius (see chapter 3 below), which was designed to be read by those who have no Greek and who would find the usual translations no more intelligible than Greek. I think I may claim that my purpose is, in a humbler way, the same as that of the learned and pious author of that translation.

'Why read the Fathers?' is a respectable question, as any theological student, harried by his tutors and bemused by the texts of the dead languages, will tell you. My answer to such students is always that it is profitable and exciting to read the fathers, if for no more exalted reason, because in them you find the Church wrestling at a very early stage with questions that have concerned it in every generation since, and which are still concerning it now. Sometimes they are questions which the Scriptures are not designed to answer—questions subsidiary to the great controversy between God and his people, but none the less urgent questions. Nothing is lost, and I here hope something is positively gained, by returning to the early days and seeing what happened when these questions came for the first time before a learned and articulate Christian mind. I think

9

we can say that all the matters dealt with in this book are of topical interest to-day, whether they be practical or dogmatic. All of them form good subjects for discussion or for meditation. Here I present the answers given by men of the early centuries, together with comments of my own which I hope may provide material for further discussion among those who take seriously the Church's ministry of thinking.

But in any case I believe the responsible Christian is the better, and will know himself to be the better, for reading only a couple of pages of Athanasius or of Origen. When their arguments strike him as familiar, he will have his notion of the Communion of Saints confirmed and illuminated, and when they strike him as strange or unusual, he will at least know himself to be conversing with, and learning from, some of the giants of the Church's thought and devotion. I have not thought it necessary to place the chapters in the order dictated by their authors' dates; rather I have placed them in the order that their subjects seemed to make appropriate. As a result, it will often be found that one chapter leads naturally into the next.

I must explain that for the translations I take full responsibility. Other translations have in most cases been before me, but I thought it best to make my own afresh. In the case of Athanasius (as I explain in chapter 3) my translation is made almost unnecessary by the existence of a really classic modern translation. In the chapter on Basil I substitute a paraphrase which the student had better know will be of no use whatever to him as a 'crib'. But I must emphasize that, however imperfect the translations and however short my extracts necessarily have to be, I thought it best to let the authors speak for themselves; in some cases I admit that the effect may be as maddening to some readers as snippets of Beethoven or Mozart in a radio feature.

It must be added, however, that should any reader be moved by these pages to browse among the Fathers, he will find all he wants (for the first ten years anyhow) in the admirable series, *The Library of Christian Classics*, published in Great Britain by the S.C.M. Press, and in the United States of America by the Westminster Press. All the first eight volumes, which cover the period dealt with here, are available. The whole is in English, and the translations are always good.

For a good deal of what I say here the reader will have to take my word; I have thought it best not to footnote every sentence, and to dispense with most of the apparatus proper to a work designed to enhance its author's reputation as a scholar. I am writing this primarily for younger people, to provide an introduction, however sketchy and tentative, for those who would not otherwise have encountered it, to the wisdom of the Fathers.

I

ORIGEN

On Reading the Bible

Origenes, born 185, head of the Catechetical School in Alexandria, died a martyr in the persecution of Valerian, 253. Date of work quoted, about 230.

THERE is no more effective inspirer of discussion, particularly among young Christians, than the question, 'How should we read the Bible?'. We are all familiar with the very pious persons whose conversation is largely composed of quotations from Scripture; with the 'lifemen' who apply the closure to religious discussions by quoting First John; with the wild men of religion who terrify their children with tales of hell, chiefly quoted from the Book of Revelation, and who keep their wives short of housekeeping by extravagant gifts to religious causes, justifying themselves from a passage in Leviticus and carefully avoiding St Mark 7. Dr Grensted, when he was Nolloth Professor at Oxford, entertained a class one day with the story of a soldier who said he did not approve of pacifism because 'The Bible says, "He maketh wars"'. You cannot move very far along the Christian way without discovering that there must be a large number of wrong ways of reading the Bible; you may well be led to think that the Bible is a remarkably difficult book, and that you had better not try to understand it.

Myself, I doubt whether it is ever wise to tell Christian believers that the Bible is a difficult book; and yet paradoxically it is never wise to let them feel that there are no difficulties about reading the Bible. Of course, difficulties themselves are part of the ordinary texture of life. The real trouble is, not that the Bible (or anything else) is difficult, but that people are difficult. It is possible to make honest mistakes about the Bible, and it is comparatively easy to correct them, and no harm done; but it is also possible to make deliberate mistakes about it, to fall into error which is the direct consequence of our own refusal to see anything in it but what we expected to find there, or what will prove that something we have just said is right. That is a much more serious matter.

However—we are concerned here with honest intellectual questions about the Bible which anybody is entitled to ask. And we introduce Origen because he was the first person to come forward with a straight answer to the honest intellectual question.

Let us look about us and see how many-sided is the grace that comes to different people from the Bible. To hear some learned persons talking you would gather (to do them justice, they would not want you to gather: but you would gather) that it is impossible for an unlearned person ever to read the Bible without falling into one trap after another, and being misled time after time. What with the fallibility of translators, the corruption of original texts, the caprices of ancient editors, the repetitions and contradictions which the somewhat ham-handed efforts of priestly scribes of the early days have left in the story, you may wonder how you are ever to find anything in the Bible that you can trust. And yet experience shows that that is miles away from the facts. There are hundreds of thousands of simple and godly folk who never heard a lecture 'on the Bible', and who never read a line of the Moffatt Commentary, in whose lives a daily Bible reading bears fruit that nobody can gainsay. How in the world do those people get through Leviticus and I Chronicles and the 109th Psalm without laying the Book down and saying, 'No, this is no use to me'? By what strange alchemy do these folk transform the bloody cruelty of Kings and the intricate counterpoint of II Cor. 1 into material that simply enriches the texture of a simple and religious life? And all this when our pulpits are frequently un-biblical or even anti-biblical, and our system of teaching the common folk about the Bible is so obviously creaky and inefficient at many points—it really is a profound and gracious mystery.

You will not by-pass the problem by saying, 'Ah, well: ignorance is bliss.' You cannot dismiss your old-fashioned faithful Bible-reader as ignorant and uneducated, or you will be led to the quaint conclusion that ignorance and lack of education are in themselves part of the good life. It is not the ignorance that works the miracle: it is something positive, not the absence of something. It is, as a matter of fact, something we are going to be discussing in our second chapter, but for the present we may be content to say that it is simply faith.

We may well feel alarmed and sorry that the habit of simple and disciplined Bible-reading has so largely disappeared from Christian homes. The simple Bible-reader I have here introduced is a real person, but at this time of day he is likely to be an elderly person, or a person now dead but lovingly remembered. What we have now is, on the one hand, numbers of people who though they are believing Christians never open their Bibles even in church;

and on the other, a devoted few who wrestle with the Scriptures with the help of commentaries learned or popular, whose chief effect is to show them what difficulties they are up against. We stand to-day in crying need of the kind of commentary which will really illuminate the *mind* of Scripture, instead of doing little more than drawing attention to its difficulties: the kind of commentary that Matthew Henry wrote in 1700, which, when you read it, causes you quite soon to put the commentary down and return to the Bible, because you realize in a new way that the Bible is an urgent and relevant book.

Now Origen, the greatest mind among all the early Fathers of the Church, has something topical to say about the reading of the Bible. I take him to be one of the most audacious minds that have ever adorned the Church's doctrine. Had he lived in this modern age he would have been swamped and suffocated with publicity. The eager clamour of press and radio nowadays is enough to extinguish this kind of person under a swarm of invitations to speak at study groups. But Origen's mind was brave enough for the Church of later times always to have some doubts about his trustworthiness. Here and there he went too far : but the Church would have been much the poorer if Origen had not made his hundred great gestures against 'safe' theology.

He wrote voluminously : he lived in a time which was peaceful enough to allow him to do so. He came from Alexandria, and when he was in his 'teens a considerable persecution of Christians broke out in that city, which had the effect of raising his enthusiasm for the Faith to an almost feverish pitch. But nothing further of the kind happened for nearly forty years, and when it did happen, he fell a martyr to it. He was primarily a philosopher, and the passage to which we are going to attend comes from the early part of a philosophical treatise entitled *De Principiis* ('The Principles of Religion').

'Taking the Scriptures literally,' he says in general effect, 'is having a disastrous effect on Christendom. People are either reading them in blind credulity, or they are being put off them altogether by their difficulty; and some ingenious people are cutting through the difficulties by placing quite fanciful interpretations on the text.' Then he selects a few passages from Scripture, and says to his reader in effect, 'What do you really think this means? Are you taking the whole of it literally? Well, let us see what happens if you do. Or are you expecting to be edified? Then let us see what you have to do with it in order to be edified. Take the story of Lot's intercourse with his daughter, or the story of the elaborate trappings of the Tabernacle in Exodus 35. Is that either edifying or true? What about the command in the Sermon on the Mount to offer your left cheek if somebody strikes you first on the right? Unless he be left-handed it is your left cheek that he will strike first.Why is it supposed that your right eye is more likely to be the cause of offence than your left eye? When our Lord said "Greet no man by the way", did he there mean Christians to adopt a surly and unsociable manner?'

That comes in Book 4, chapter 19 of the *De Principiis*—and, of course, anybody can do that kind of thing. Take the text of the Bible and isolate this or that passage, and you can always make it look ridiculous. Origen's purpose, however, is to show people the vitally important truth that as a matter of fact nobody ever does read the Bible dead literally. Well then, if we are already exercising the right of interpretation, and are not approaching the Bible with the slavish literalness proper to *Bradshaw*, we had better examine the principles we work on.

From here, let him speak for himself. Origen's Greek is by no means J. B. Phillips's English, and it is tough going; but here is the gist of it.

De Principiis 4 : 20-21

These arguments are designed to show that we do less than justice to that divine power which gave us the sacred writings if we interpret them merely according to the letter, for, as we have seen, we shall now and again come across passages which, taken literally, say what is untrue, or absurd, or impossible. We have further shown that frequently historic narrative and valuable precept are interwoven. But I hope nobody will think that, because some events recorded as historic are not historic, therefore I am saying that no biblical history is trustworthy; or that because here and there we find a precept which, taken literally, leaves us with absurdity or impossibility, I would urge that no scriptural precept is worth our attention. I should not dream of saying that what eye-witnesses have written about our Saviour is false, or that none of his teaching is to be attended to. No—on the contrary, we must say that in many matters the sacred writings speak the plain historic truth. We need not doubt that Abraham

was buried in the great tomb at Hebron, and after him
Isaac and Jacob and their wives, or that Sichem was
given to Joseph as his portion (Gen. 25.9; 48.22; Josh.
24.32). We need not doubt that Jerusalem is the capital
city of Judaea, where Solomon built a temple to the
Lord. In a thousand places Scripture may be historically
trusted. Indeed, those places where plain historic truth
is recorded are more numerous than those whose force
lies rather in the underlying spiritual message. Similarly, nobody will seriously doubt that the command,
'Love thy father and thy mother' is valid and to be
observed without any mystical interpretation: why,
the apostle Paul uses the very same expression. Need
we make any further comment on 'Thou shalt do no
murder', 'Thou shalt not steal', 'Thou shalt not commit adultery', 'Thou shalt not bear false witness'?
There are injunctions written in the Gospel in respect
of which we need never ask whether they should be
taken literally or not, such as where it is written, 'I
say unto you, that whosoever is angry with his
brother . . .' and 'I say unto you, swear not at all'
(Matt. 5.22, 34). We may unconditionally observe what
the apostle enjoins, 'Warn them that are unruly, com-
fort the feeble-minded, support the weak, be patient
toward all men' (I Thess. 5.14)—even though the
pedantic may wish to urge that the depths of God's
wisdom could save every one of the Thessalonians
apart from the literal observance of these precepts.

None the less, the man of careful mind will encounter
perplexity, on those occasions when he cannot see for

himself without close examination whether a supposed
history is or is not history, and whether an injunction
is or is not literally binding. Therefore the reader will
do well to recall our Lord's words, 'Search the scriptures' (John 5.39),[1] and carefully examine where the
literal meaning is the true meaning, and where it cannot
be. He must investigate, so far as he can, by examination of similar sayings, the 'mind of Scripture', that is,
the principle of all Scripture, when he encounters a
saying that cannot be taken literally. Then he will find
that, although the series of words under review taken
literally yields an impossible sense, the leading thought
is not only not impossible but positively true. He must
strive to apprehend the whole meaning, carefully com-
paring the difficult passage with other passages where
the same expression leaves us with a possible and true
sense, and he will find that these other passages join
their force with the one that seemed to be impossible,
to yield a spiritual sense. We must never forget that not
all Scripture bears a 'physical' meaning, but all bears
a 'spiritual' meaning; that is obvious from our demonstration of the well-known fact that the 'physical'
meaning sometimes yields an impossible sense. In sum,
then, the reader should bring close attention to bear,
that he may properly meet the sacred books as the
writings of God. We have sufficiently explained our
own view on the character of writing that he may
expect to find in them.

[1] The Fathers seem to agree in reading John 5.39 thus; but
modern authorities (e.g. A.R.S.V.) urge us to read 'You search the
scriptures' (sc. 'but you do not understand them rightly').

A few comments on this will serve to make clear its chief contentions.

First : Origen's systematic answer to the question of how the Bible is to be read is to say that every passage of the Bible may be read in one or more of three different ways. These he calls the 'physical', the 'moral' and the 'spiritual' ways of reading. The 'physical' way is to read quite literally. That is to say, to read the passage as though it had been written yesterday, and means exactly what it would have meant yesterday. While he is careful to admit that much of the Bible may be read like that, he contends that not all of it can be so read, and that so to read passages which have lost their literal sense, or which never had any literal sense, is not merely to miss the point but to damage your faith, because it may lead you to say that Scripture is just not to be trusted. At an earlier point he gives Gen. 49.10 as a good example of a passage which never had any literal sense; and indeed that passage has been a happy hunting ground for textual critics ever since, and regularly appears in university examination papers still. Other passages which actually make sense but do not make literal sense include both those like the cheek-turning passage whose meaning is obvious but not quite literal, and those which leave us with a morally or historically impossible conclusion. The imprecatory psalms are examples of moral difficulty, and Ex. 35-39 contains much that is historically impossible. Your faith, Origen would say, will be damaged if you are unable to deal rightly with a psalm of hatred : either you will think that that is laid down by Scripture as the right way for a godly man to think and act, or you will say, 'If Scripture enjoins that I pray for the throwing of Babylonian children's heads against the stones, how can I ever trust Scripture?' Either you will not notice the inconsistency between the 'tabernacle of meeting' in its simple form in the older stratum of Exodus and the enormously elaborate structure described in its last chapters, or noticing it you will say 'This story makes no sense'.

The moral interpretation of Scripture does not actually appear in our extract, and Origen devotes little time to it elsewhere, presumably because he thinks that once you see the point it hardly needs explanation. It chiefly concerns narratives which may not be strictly historical but which clearly have a moral import that is unassailable. Modern critics might speak thus of Gen. 3: it is acceptably said nowadays that, never mind whether the tale is historically factual, its moral import is absolutely crucial in the whole story of our Redemption.

But the 'spiritual' interpretation of Scripture is that which Origen is chiefly concerned to bring to our notice, and our extract contains the chief clues to our understanding of that. The 'spiritual' interpretation, through allegory or through what is technically called *anagogy*,[1] can often lead us to the heart of the matter. Origen does not go very deeply into the difference between allegory and anagogy; we have St Thomas Aquinas to thank for that. The difference is this: allegory is the hiding of familiar but important truths under a story which may be fictional or legendary, and allegorical interpretation is treating stories which will not bear historic scrutiny under the assumption that they do conceal familiar but important truths. Anagogy is the more particular device of concealing within some such story a clear truth about God's dealings with his people. It is sometimes put thus, that in anagogy in the Old Testa-

---

[1] It may help the reader if we say that this hideous word is normally pronounced with its third syllable long, as in 'goat', not as in 'log'.

ment we may find, if we look carefully, a prophetic reference to Christ. But it is equally proper to say that in anagogy
we find a clue to the whole system by which God created,
redeemed, and supports his people. It is, broadly, the
difference between a general truth concealed in the passage
and a specifically Christian or evangelical truth. To take
Gen. 3 as an example: if you are reading it and say, 'I now
know that in a certain year one Adam and one Eve ate a
fruit off a tree and displeased God by so doing', you are
taking it literally. If you say, 'I now know that it is wrong
to disobey the commands of God', you are taking it
morally. If you say, 'Adam and Eve are mankind and the
trees of the garden are the devices by which man hides
from God, and the flaming sword is the barrier between
man and happiness placed there because of man's disobedience', you are taking it allegorically. If you say, 'I
now know that in the redemption wrought in Christ there
are the memory of disobedience, the wrath and compassion
of God, and the continuing deceit of man to be reckoned
with', you are taking it anagogically. But let it be remembered that the allegorical and the anagogic methods were
not fully distinguished by Origen, though he uses the Greek
for both words. On the whole he disliked allegory, and
when he says 'allegorical' he usually means what St
Thomas distinguished as 'anagogic'.

He goes on to say that none of Scripture is meaningless,
although not all of it can be interpreted literally. He would
have agreed that this is because some of it is intentionally
legend, tradition or poetry rather than history, and some of
it belongs to another age morally or linguistically: we
should now add that some of it survives only in hopelessly
corrupt texts.

But, for the second of our large points, Origen insists

that the secret of profitable Bible-reading is the discovery
of the 'mind' of Scripture (*nous*). Recall how he says that
if you are in difficulty it is well to interpret the passage by
some other parallel passage that says the same thing in a
general way but is not difficult in the same way. Take for
example that famous moral 'crux', Psalm 137.7-9. Literally
it won't do: dashing children's heads against the stones, no
matter what the circumstances, is indefensible. Then go to
some other part of the Bible and learn what the background
situation was. 'Babylon' is the clue—the dark years in
which that powerful enemy captured Jerusalem and
deported a number of the most eminent, and therefore the
most religious, people of Jerusalem to live in the suburbs of
Babylon, a heathen city. Jeremiah will give the atmosphere
of that time (Jer. 7; 13.20-27; 15.5-10; and 29, for example).
Or read the Lamentations, which express the grief of the
religious Jew over the catastrophe. That is the grief, boil-
ing over into hatred, behind Psalm 137. Here is a man
separated from everything that is dear to him, a religious
patriot who has lost his home and his church. Then you
can say of Psalm 137—'By the waters of Babylon we sat
down and wept'—yes, they may well have done (*literal*).
'If I forget thee, O Jerusalem, let my right hand forget her
cunning'—here speaks a musician (*literal*); he would rather
have his right hand paralysed than forget his God in a
heathen country (*literal*)—so may I never forget my God
(*moral*). 'Happy shall he be that taketh and dasheth thy
little ones against the stones'—so may I as a Christian
grieve over the consequences of sin, and so may I be wrath-
ful against the Father of Lies (*spiritual*). The anagogic
reading here would be the denial of the spirit of revenge
by Christ, and the drawing off into his suffering of all that
poison in the world's system which produced, in that par-

ticular case, the horrors of the deportation and the revenge-
ful spirit of the deportees. Anagogy, by the way, may be
contradicted by the Gospel, but it never stops there. For
the divine contradiction of sin is redemption.

Thus we may 'search the scriptures', and seek especially
for the *mind* of Scripture.

Now see how fruitful that can become when we confront
passages which might have presented little difficulty to
Origen, but which present considerable diffculty to modern
people. Consider the miracles of Christ. To many intelligent
men of the modern world they still present a real
stumbling-block. 'That sort of thing can't happen', we
say, and therefore we must either disbelieve the stories or
look on our Lord as a magician who took advantage of his
powers at times, and at other times, for example on the
cross, inexplicably refused to use them. You may or may
not be helped if we say that it is dogmatically a sign of
Christ's divinity that he could do these things, or that most
of the 'miracles' could nowadays be paraphrased by
psychology or chemistry. It is likely that neither of these
lines will do you much good. Ask first the question, 'Now,
what is the story that all Scripture is telling?' Then ask,
'What is the total picture of Christ that comes to us
through those passages of the Gospels—the vast majority—
about which there need be no reasonable doubt?' In the
answers to those questions you will certainly encounter the
truth about man's sin and hatred of the good, God's design
to rescue man from his situation without enslaving him,
and the obedience and humility of Christ. You will deduce,
about Christ, that whatever else may be true, he was never
incompetent, never inconsistent, and never given to self-
display. Whatever you say about the healing of lepers and
blind men must be within that known framework; so must

anything you say about the Gadarene swine and the barren
fig-tree. It is not my business here to offer expositions of
those passages;[1] but these are the clues we may profitably
follow. We shall be returning to this subject in chapter 3.

But Origen is never a mere don, never a dehumanized
pedant. He has always an eye on the simple believer with
whom we began this chapter. What is the simple believer's
secret? Why, surely, that it has been given to him to understand the mind of Scripture, by revelation from God. You
can come at much of it by hard searching; but if you do it
by hard searching you must expect painful wrestling and
constant rebuke and contradiction by the Word of God.
Most of us are in that position to-day. To some—and it
matters not whether they are educated or learned—it is
given to accept Christ's redemption without, like Thomas,
investigating the wounds. You will find that anybody who
fits our (and Origen's) description of the 'simple believer'
is a person who has apprehended the mind of Scripture.
Such a person, reading Psalm 137, will not react violently
and say, 'I don't understand this; I disagree with it; therefore I reject it;' nor will he say, like some two-dimensional
mole-like creature, 'I am here permitted to be vengeful'.
He will simply say, because he is in the habit of saying,
'God is saying something here, and I will wait until I hear
it. What it says will be above my reach, not below it, and
I will not limit the word of God to the reach of my own
mind.' That attitude has the texture of faith. This, in the
end, is the secret, whether you be learned or unlearned, of
the friendliness of the Bible.

[1] I have attempted to do so in my book, *The Gift of Conversion*
(Lutterworth, 1957).

2

CLEMENT OF ALEXANDRIA

On Faith and Knowledge

Titus Flavius Clemens, born about 150, head of the Catechetical School in Alexandria, died about 215. Date of work quoted: about 210.

ɪ F you have ever witnessed an encounter between a man who says, 'I can't prove it, but I believe it', and another who says, 'Then if you can't prove it, it is of no use to me,' you have been present at a part of the controversy in which Clement of Alexandria played a leading part. The question before us here will be : What part has knowledge, and what part has education, in the make-up of a man's Christian faith? Nobody can deny that, in an age so saturated with knowledge and information as our own age is, that is a question of enormous importance. So we will go to second-century Alexandria and see what they made of it there.

You will not be too badly misled if you imagine Alexandria as a place carrying in the ancient world a reputation not unlike that which Liverpool has among the British. Alexandria was, as it still is, a focal point of Mediterranean culture and trade. Its population consisted basically of native Africans, Arabs, and Greeks, the Greeks being descendants of Macedonian colonists who, by A.D. 150, had sent down deeper roots into Alexandrian culture than those of the passing traders or of the Roman governors. Alexandria was known as one of the roughest populations in the Mediterranean world—good for a riot at any time on very little provocation. Athanasius, who lived there most of his life, could tell some stories about the race-gangs of Alexandria. To the serious-minded sociologist, the author, as it were, of *Alexandrian Life and Leisure*, the city would appear as a mass of corruption lightly topped by a strident and impudent vulgarity. But Alexandria had its university as well as its dockside. It had a university which above all others of the ancient world was renowned for progressive philosophy. It had more than one famous library. One is thought by some (but others deny it) to have been burnt down by Julius Caesar, but Tertullian (about A.D. 200) mentions another in the reverent terms which learned men of England reserve for the British Museum or the Bodleian. Alexandrian philosophy was, in these early centuries, the most adventurously speculative of any; it was from this school that outside the Christian circle came the mighty names of Philo (fl. A.D. 50) and of Plotinus and Porphyry (both of the early third century).

Within the academic circle there grew up a Christian college, known to historians as the Catechetical School, which numbered amongst its presidents Titus Flavius Clemens, commonly called Clement, and his successor Origen. It is clear that from the earliest days of its work, this theological college of Alexandria was the place where Greek philosophy of a still developing kind and Christianity of that vital brand which only North Africa could produce in those days met each other and fertilized each other. Very orthodox people were always saying 'What in the world are these fellows at Alexandria going to say next?' Those who took very literally the Pauline aphorism that

the Faith is foolishness to the Greeks, and thought that no
terms could be made between Christianity and contemporary culture, found great offence in what went on in the
college whose president was Clement.

But whether you (whom I am supposing to be an
ordinary second-century Christian for the moment) cared
for it or not, every educated man in those days was a
Hellenist; every man who had learned to handle books and
ideas, every man who had investigated the machinery of
thinking and learned how to operate it, had been brought
up on Greek literature, Greek philosophy, Greek logic.
There were other literatures, other philosophies; but either
a man would approach these through Greek teaching
methods, or they would belong to the non-intellectual part
of his life—to that part of life which is concerned with not
spilling the salt and not walking under ladders. Therefore
the encounter with Greek philosophy was no merely
academic concern for the Christian. It was the question,
' What has speculation and knowledge to do with Christ? '
that was being asked. ' Is it the same faculty that knows
God and that knows Greek? Is the developing of the Greek-
knowing faculty going to help or to hinder the growth of
the God-knowing faculty? ' Other places answered this
differently, but Alexandria said, ' There is no real conflict.
Christianity and culture can be friends. Christianity is not
a religion for the illiterate and the irresponsible.'

Now when we have to do with Cyprian (chh. 5-6) we
shall see that this view had its disagreeable consequences.
It did encourage a religion in some people that was broad
rather than deep; it did bring into the church business men
and intellectuals and men of letters who accepted church
membership without seriously considering what happened
when Christianity encountered elements in ' culture ' which

contradicted it and vilified it. In consequence, such people broke down under persecution and accepted Caesar's word when it was backed by force against Christ's word which could only be backed by virtue. Tertullian, also an African, but a very different kind of African from Clement or Origen, wrote that philosophy is the devil's business, because his insights were always concerned with the points where Christianity came into head-on collision with secular notions and practices.

It depended very much on what kind of person you were whether you appreciated Clement of Alexandria. Probably it still does. For some he was (and is) much too agreeable, too far gone in senior-common-room urbanity. Red-hot zealots for the purity of doctrine would say, 'It's all very well for him in his study: he wouldn't talk like that if he had my congregation to deal with every day.' For example: when Clement said that in the end God is the Absolute and the Indescribable, that you can only speak of him in negative epithets, so far is he above our comprehension, the practical Christian says, 'That is too cold; too vague; a God like that can't help me.' And the biblical Christian says, 'The Bible tells me to think of God as a Father; it even permits me to think of him as a Lover; but I don't find anything there about the Absolute.' The theologian might say, 'Clement is, at that point, a neoplatonist who has no Hebraic insight.' Quite so—that is the stuff of legitimate controversy. Clement has all the weakness of the man who loves books almost too much; and yet we must admit that in this reluctance to describe the Most High God, this hesitation to claim familiarity with him, there is a certain seemly reverence which is very far from being sub-Christian, and against which it is possible for the very zealous to offend. It is an intellectual 'Depart from me' which, even if it does not chime with this or that man's experience, should not be undervalued by any who would take a generous view of the majesty of the Christian mysteries.

Clement brings to his theological teaching and argument an unsurpassed classical equipment. More than any other Christian thinker of the early time he knew his Greek and Latin authors, the poets and historians as well as the philosophers. In the work from which we are going to take a quotation, he quotes from well over five hundred different authors; and he is concerned all the time to show that Christianity is not the denial but the crown of classical culture.

To demonstrate that would take more space than we have here. We shall do better to go straight to the central point, which is, I believe, the question whether knowledge (by which he allows himself to mean not only learning and information but also the mental equipment by which it is made use of) is in the Christian race an advantage or a burden. Is knowledge, is the whole intellectual system, one of the things which the disciple who travels light, in the manner of Matt. 10.10, must leave behind? Is it easier for a camel to pass through a needle's eye than for a man of culture to enter the Kingdom? That is the question. Now we will attend to two passages from Clement's *Miscellanies* (in the original, *Stromateis*).

Stromateis 7.55 and 60

Insight is, so to put it, a kind of perfection in man, a completion of his human nature; for it is brought to fulfilment, through the knowledge of sacred things, in terms of his behaviour, his manner of life, and his conversation. It is always harmonious and consistent both in itself and with the word of God. Since the man of faith becomes complete in this way alone, we can say that it is through insight that 'faith is made perfect' (James 2.22). Faith is, as it were, a virtue of inward disposition; it both confesses the being of God, and glorifies him in his being without any searching for God. It is here that a man must begin, and then, increasing in faith by God's grace, he will attain, so far as he is able, insight concerning God. I say that insight must be distinguished from the wisdom that is imparted by teaching. Whatever can be called insight can also be called wisdom, but not all that is wisdom can be called insight. The very form of the word for wisdom (*sophia*) derives from the activity of retaining the uttered word, that is, from memory.[1] But the foundation of insight is in having no doubt about God, that is, in believing. Wisdom looks back to what has been learnt; insight looks forward to what is promised. Christ is both the foundation of wisdom and the dwelling-place of insight. In him are the beginning and the end of the whole process. From the human point of view the beginning is in faith and the end is in love, the middle term, insight, being handed on by tradition, like an inheritance, to those who according to God's grace show themselves worthy of the teaching; and as a result of teaching the

[1] This is a very far-fetched Greek conceit that makes no sense in English and precious little in Greek; it is derived from a passage in Plato's *Cratylus* (412B), and does not matter at all to us provided that we accept the movement of the argument, which is to distinguish acquired wisdom from natural insight.

dignity of love shines forth in increasing brilliance. 'To him that hath it shall be given'—insight added to faith, love to insight, and to love, the inheritance of glory. . . .

The man of insight, then, has a large and generous notion of the universe, because he has mastered divine doctrine. As Plato says, he 'begins from an attitude of wonder' towards the creation,[1] and that attitude makes him from the beginning a good learner of the Lord; and as soon as he hears of God and of his providence his 'wonder' moves him to belief. Beginning there, he makes every effort towards learning, and does everything which will make him able to achieve the insight he longs for; as faith deepens, the longing and the seeking together increase; and the thing he longs for is precisely to become worthy of such exalted and noble contemplation. And so the man of insight is at the disposal of the truths revealed by the words he learns. A commandment, for example, such as 'Thou shalt not commit adultery' he understands not as it presents itself to people at large, but with special insight, because the words convey to him the hidden realities within them, and the duties they enjoin make their demands not merely of his outward ears but of his whole self.

On this passage there are two large comments to be made. The first begins at the linguistic level, and leads up from there. When we write 'insight' and 'the man of insight', we are translating a word of crucial importance in the original. The word for 'insight' in the Greek is

[1] Probably *Theaetetus* 155.

gnosis, and the word for 'the man of insight' is *gnostikos*. And as soon as you mention that word, 'gnostic', you are pitched into the middle of one of the great ancient religious controversies. It was a point of controversy because 'Gnosticism' was a word of very special meaning among the ancient Christians. To use any word cognate with 'Gnostic' was to appear to ally yourself with a whole religious outlook which Christians were bound to regard as highly suspect. Something of the same kind, on a smaller scale, has happened in modern times with the word 'Evangelical'; it is a perfectly innocent English word meaning 'pertaining to the Gospel'; but in common religious speech we know well that we use the word to describe a way of thinking about the Bible and the Atonement which is not universally accepted among Christians. It was worse with 'gnosticism', which is equally a perfectly innocent Greek word meaning 'knowledge', because, while nobody thinks of 'the Evangelicals' as a heresy undeserving of the name 'Christian', Gnosticism is certainly a heresy. It is a compendious name for an enormous complex of oriental religions concerning which the new Faith of Christ had to find how much it could concede and how much it must resist. Now you will understand Clement if you think of him rather as you would think of a modern Christian who seeks to rescue the word 'evangelical' from its technical meaning by saying, 'I hold neither of those special views which "Evangelicals" profess; but, take it or leave it, I'm an evangelical.' Just so Clement would have said, 'I subscribe to none of the queer doctrines and practices of Gnosticism; but I'm a gnostic.' He means, of course, that it is still possible to make an important point in Christian thinking by using the word 'gnosis' in an innocent way.

But of course the suspicion of Gnosticism was well

founded, and if we glance at it for a moment, we shall see just how important it was for somebody to make the point that Clement is making. Gnosticism of this or that kind is a perversion of Christianity which it is well to be on our guard against. Native Gnosticism—Gnosticism among people who do not pretend to be Christians—is one thing; Gnosticism masquerading as Christianity is quite another. Books of five hundred pages have been written about Gnosticism, but if we are to give in a few lines a notion of what it was in Gnosticism that the early Christians thought dangerous, it was a quality that showed itself in two principles. The first of these was that there is an inner ring of religious people who are enabled, in virtue of their initiation, to see the truth that is denied to people at large; the second is that all matter is contemptible, and that the God of true religion (in Christian Gnosticism, the God of the New Testament) had nothing to do with creation. Created matter was formed by a subordinate deity after the principle of evil and negation had made itself manifest, and is therefore irrecoverably tainted with that principle of evil and negation. One could go on to describe the complicated and barbarous systems of belief and practice that emerged from these principles, and the astonishing diversity of outward form that Gnostic worship and faith took, from the comparatively innocent to the downright obscene. But for the ordinary Christian believer in the second century or the twentieth it is sufficient simply to say, 'Where you find a religion at whose heart there is contempt, there you find a false religion.' For you can see that the two principles mentioned above share the taint of contempt—the 'inner ring' principle being a manifestation of contempt of people, and the 'damnation of matter' principle being a manifestation of contempt of things. And it is easy to see in later history religious aberrations which sound the Gnostic note very clearly. There was in classic Gnosicism usually a preoccupation with the supernatural or ideal world, an obsessive theorizing about those orders of being which insulated the perfection of God from the corruption of Creation. It is not difficult to detect a Gnostic flavour in the complex ideal systems of such thinkers as Emanuel Swedenborg, or in the accent of the kind of modern religion (to be found amongst people of all denominations) which prefers high thoughts to redemption and J. G. Whittier to Isaac Watts. Christian opinion in the early centuries reacted to all this as violently as Christian opinion should react to the superior and the highbrow, to the people whose religion makes them say 'Are you one of us?' and the people who misuse the word 'spiritual'. And I am ready to suspect that then, just as now, it was not only that the Gnostic kind of doctrine had its attractions, but that the people who professed Gnosticism were often so gentle and cultivated in their ways, that made great diffi- culties for the Christian apologist.

Now a reading of the passage we quoted shows well enough that Clement expressed himself in a way that made some think that he was tarred with this brush. But if we listen to his words and follow his argument, we shall find that although he sails near the wind, although he is 'living dangerously' in his characteristically Alexandrian way, he is not in any heretical sense a Gnostic. His statements of classic Christian doctrines often reveal an approach unusual in a primitive Christian, but he never abandons the doctrines. The heretical part of Gnosticism was in that it denied the fact and therefore the grace of the Incarna- tion. Clement was no George MacLeod, but he never came within a hundred miles of denying the Incarnation.

But here we are discussing the process that he calls *gnosis*, and which we have interpreted in the word 'insight'. And this leads to our second comment.

I think that, if we dismiss all the peripheral considerations about whether Clement was or was not a Gnostic of the unpleasant sort, we need find no difficulty in seeing what he is about. His language is a little obscure, because he does not always use a given word to mean the same thing. In paragraph 55 (the first of the two in the quotation) he is distinguishing between insight and knowledge. Now the Greek for the knowledge that he places below insight is *sophia*, always a word of exalted connotation in Greek. The wise man, the *sophos*, in Plato and the philosophers generally, is the man who is within sight of the *summum bonum*. Paul is content to describe the grace of the cross as the 'power and the wisdom of God', the *dynamis* and the *sophia*. This makes it difficult to use 'wisdom' in any derogatory sense, to claim that at the intellectual level anything is higher. It is difficult, but it is just that that Clement is doing. We should almost certainly say 'wisdom is higher than knowledge' and the Greek for that would be '*sophia* is higher than *gnosis*'. But Clement turns the whole system inside-out by saying that in effect there is a kind of knowledge which is higher than wisdom.

When an ingenious parson is suddenly seized with the original and daring thought that modern technology has overtaken modern moral progress, he is saying something like Clement is saying, but at a lower level. He is moralizing with the distinction between wisdom and knowledge; but Clement wants to do more. The secret is that although Clement was a classic to the backbone, he was not ignorant of his Bible, nor by any means uninfluenced by its thought; and we can hardly doubt that he had noticed what a singular weight of meaning the Scriptures gives to the verb 'I know'. It is used in the Bible of relations of the greatest intimacy. You have it in the expression 'He knew his wife', and again in 'Know the Lord'. So far as I can discover, Clement does not quote Jeremiah 31.31-4 in any of his philosophical works: but what he is saying in paragraph 55 is not far from the promise recorded in Jeremiah, where it is written that in God's purpose the time will come when men shall not teach one another about the Lord, but shall all *know* the Lord. Clement, we see, is saying that wisdom imparted by teaching is one thing, but insight is something more, including the reverent acceptance of teaching, but adding faith.

The difficulty comes when he says that 'insight' can be handed on by tradition. At this point a celebrated translator whose edition,[1] among others, is before me as I write, no longer translates *gnosis* by 'insight' but calls it simply 'knowledge'. But I think that Clement's meaning must be this: that since *gnosis* presupposes that those who have it are worthy to receive it, those who have had it in every age form a circle of faithful souls of whom it makes sense to say that those of one generation have handed it on to those of another. But in the main the paragraph is certainly saying that just as faith and love cannot be taught (only, at best, inculcated by example), but must be living qualities of their possessors, so neither can insight be taught. It would have been simpler, and I think it would have come to the same thing, to say that the part of *gnosis* that can be taught is *sophia*. At one point Clement makes insight a middle term between faith and love. But his real meaning is slightly obscured by that; for what he really means surely

[1] F. J. A. Hort and J. B. Mayor, *Clement of Alexandria, Miscellanies, Book VII* (Macmillan, 1902).

is that insight is wisdom plus the theological virtues—faith, hope and charity. And if he says that, he comes right back to I Cor. 13, in which we have faith, hope and charity simply leading to the great consummation, 'then shall I know even as I am known'.

Paragraph 60 amplifies this in a strikingly evangelical way. Here you have all the strength as well as all the weakness of Clement's spiritual technique. The weakness—the point where he lays himself open to the charge of technical Gnosticism—is of course where he talks about insights that are not given to the world at large, but only to the man of faith. But the point he is positively making is that the 'man of insight' is in the end distinguished not by reaching a certain achievement, but by being a certain kind of person. He begins from wonder (or admiration: a mixture of both); that is the point. He begins from a kind of love, a kind of desire towards the truth. He cannot walk this way if he begins from an attitude of complete scepticism. He knows *a priori* that there is something there for him to come at; and he loves it. The process of 'learning' which is the diversification of *gnosis* along the road of time, is a process which he enjoys; it is the fulfilment of his desire, as satisfactory as the appeasement of hunger or thirst.

'Thus,' says Clement, such a man will 'taste God's will'. But then he says something which is even more illuminating. What are we to suppose he means when he says that such a man has an understanding of the Commandments denied to other people? I myself cannot avoid the conjecture that he is here reaching right forward to that remarkable seventeenth-century treatise, *The Marrow of Modern Divinity* (two parts, 1645 and 1648), whose arguments can adequately be summarized in words from its own text, 'Moses heard the Commandments not only from Mount

Sinai, but from Mount Sion'. *The Marrow* is very largely concerned with an exposition of the Ten Commandments in Christian terms, and its whole purpose is to show in what way the Christian, by being a Christian, gains an understanding of the Commandments that is denied to Jews and to any others who have not the Faith. When our Lord said, in the course of his teaching, both that he came not to destroy but to fulfil the Law, and that the Pharisaic interpretations of the Law were wholly misconceived, what was he saying but that in him we have a knowledge (an intimate knowledge, a *gnosis*) of the Law denied to those who do not accept him? Or that in the light of his teaching and his work the heart of the Law is laid bare, where before we had only the letter? *The Marrow* says, and Clement would certainly have agreed, that many who came before Christ had this knowledge. It says that Moses had it. Clement would want to say that Plato had it, that in the classical philosophers and poets and dramatists there is a proleptic apprehension of the 'heart of the law' just as much as there is in the saints of the Old Testament. But both would agree that in the days before Christ, or in cultures that have not Christ, there is no 'open vision', no reliable interpretation, no spiritual authority that goes beyond the letter and can still be implicitly trusted.

You can see from the Gospels that, for example, 'Keep the Sabbath holy' means one thing to a man who has insight and another to a man who has none; it is the difference between a prohibition to be mechanically enforced, and a prohibition designed towards a positively good end. A literal interpretation of any part of 'the Law' will always be partial and misleading, but an interpretation through that 'knowledge' which is intimacy with God, and therefore intimacy with the principles on which God orders the physical and moral universe, will lead to the good life and the glory of God.

This gift of 'hearing the Law from Mount Sion', of interpreting the Law through the Gospel, is precious, but even it is not altogether beyond abuse by foolish men. Clement leaves plenty of room for its abuse. Can we say that anybody may claim, on the inward testimony of his conscience, to be a man of insight? May not that inward testimony turn out to be merely the prompting of pride? There are always liable to be Christians who say, ' I am a man of *gnosis*. I am above the common herd. Therefore the Ten Commandments don't apply to me in the same way as they apply to other people '; and he reaches for his income-tax return form and 'takes his pen and writes fifty'. It is always tempting to find reasons why the commandments either of the Old Testament or the New should not apply to ourselves when the shoe begins to pinch. This is not a question with which Clement deals. But the Puritans of the seventeenth century knew about it, and found an answer. They called these 'above the Law' people 'Antominians', and their refutation of them was always in a full clear and commanding doctrine of Grace. Insight is a gift, and all such gifts are made available by the Grace whose texture is made clear to us in the cross. To realize that when God gives, that is the way in which he gives, is to impose a sufficient moral guard against treating the gift as mere profit. To know that when God gives anything, he gives it as he gave his Son, is to guard as fully as we, being sons and not slaves, are allowed to guard against error. The gross material reality of the cross guards us from the sentimental spirituality of Gnosticism; the sheer prodigal generosity of it guards us against religious superiority.

But Clement says something very valuable when he

points the way towards an evaluation of Christian insight. Without doubt the Christian, initiated as Clement would say, converted as some of us might prefer to say, is in possession of a knowledge, an intimacy with God, which is the direct result of that initiation or conversion and which cannot be obtained by any other way. But that intimacy gives no title to contempt. It is prepared by discipline and nurtured by love of men, and it thrives on the faith which, in humble alertness, holds 'the certainty of things not seen'.[1]

[1] Heb. 11.1, translation of C. K. Williams in *The New Testament, A New Translation in Plain English* (S.P.C.K., 1952).

3

ATHANASIUS

'Death of Death, and Hell's Destruction'

Athanasius, born about 297, Patriarch of Alexandria, died 373. Date of work quoted, 318.

THESE pages would be not merely incomplete but positively misleading if they did not include some reference to the greatest, the simplest, the most vivacious and the most famous of all short theological treatises, the *De Incarnatione* of Athanasius.

Now Athanasius has this initial advantage, that his modern interpreters do full justice to his character and his work. It would be an excellent thing if I were able to refer you, in respect of any of the other figures who appear in this book, to so readable and delightful a translation of their best work as the translation of the *De Incarnatione* recently made by a religious of the Wantage Community,[1] or if I could recommend for all of them so telling a biography and character-sketch as that given of St Athanasius in the late G. L. Prestige's Bampton Lectures.[2] Both these are so good, and so much to our present purpose in being essentially good reading for those who have no specialist interest in theology, as to be almost an embarrassment to the author of such brief chapters as these. I cannot recom-

[1] *The Incarnation of the Word of God* . . . newly translated into English by a Religious of C.S.M.V. (Geoffrey Bles, 1944).
[2] G. L. Prestige, *Fathers and Heretics* (S.P.C.K., 1940), chapter 4.

43

mend either too warmly, nor too strongly urge my reader
to overcome his distrust of theological literature so far as
to get hold of them and read them for himself.

But some good will have been done if we can convey
some of the essential vitality of theology through this
brief reference to Athanasius. Too many well-intentioned
persons, not a few of them clergy and ministers, decry
theology. 'Leave it to the learned fellows in the colleges to
talk about the Three Persons and One God; plain men like
you and me must get on with the real work of life.' That is
really sorry nonsense. Sometimes it is no better than syco-
phantic cant. Why should anybody be concerned to deny
that the happiest and most desirable activity of mankind
is conversation about God? Is God a dull subject? No—the
only condition for enjoying the great felicity of talking
about God is that you attend with care to the subject, that
you use your imagination and your reason, and that you
remember that you are talking about your Father.

Perhaps the trouble is that some of us who talk about
God are dull dogs. In that case dulness comes mighty near
to treachery. Perhaps we are less in touch with material
realities than we ought to be. Perhaps we sometimes witness
to a God who could never have had the patience to make
a caterpillar or the sense of humour to have made a hippo-
potamus; to a Christ who never built chairs and tables;
to a Holy Spirit who really is the harmless gas that the
hymn-writers make him out to be. But whatever you want
to say of us, you may not say it of God, nor of theology,
nor of Athanasius.

At college they made me read Prestige's book (referred to
above), and I remember well how when I read the chapter
on Athanasius for the first time, I laid it down and said to
myself, 'What a film that story would make!' A film, I

really feel, rather than a play. There is so much movement in it, so many vivid characters. Must we say that Hollywood would inevitably vulgarize it, or may we make the bold and hazardous gesture of here and now inviting some large film corporation to dedicate all its resources to the making of a film about the Nature of God, using the hair-raising story of Athanasius? He was born about 297 and lived to be seventy-five. At twenty-one he had written the immortal work we are about to attend to; at thirty he became Patriarch of Alexandria, and during the next forty-five years he was thrown out of his see no fewer than five times—and returned five times. He lived most of the way through that turbulent fourth century when all Christendom was split across by a mighty theological controversy, during the course of which sometimes one side, sometimes the other side was in the ascendant, and if you were a prominent person on the losing side you might well fear for your liberty and even your life. Athanasius was—not to linger over the details of it—on what is normally called the ' orthodox ' side; the leader of the other side was Arius, who was claiming against Christian evidences that Jesus Christ was a creature of God, not the Son of God. To put it very broadly, Athanasius was standing for what Christians had always been saying against a careless distortion of what Christians had been saying. What his opponents wanted to substitute for the true biblical teaching about the Godhead would have had much the same effect on the subsequent history of Christian thought that you would expect if you tried, as an up-to-date innovation and as a gesture of economy, to run a car on a mixture half petrol and half water.

For bad doctrine, easy-going, lazy doctrine, is poison to the life of the church. See a church weakening, losing its grip on realities, appealing to a smaller and more exclusive class of people year by year, becoming more and more like a society of queer people, and you will always find the source of the trouble in bad doctrine and shoddy thinking. In this particular case the danger was of man's being persuaded to believe that Jesus Christ was not fully God as well as fully man; for it was easier to believe that he was either than to believe that he was both. But no good ever came of trying to bypass the difficulties and slacken the tensions that Christian doctrine presents to the mind.[1]

Athanasius, then, was the champion of the orthodox view about the Person of Christ, and in the course of his long life he hazarded everything he possessed for the vindication of the doctrine that Christ is God and Man. He suffered, and saw his friends suffer, for it, at the hands of those Alexandrian race-gangs whom we met in the last chapter. When we read the *De Incarnatione* we might well think that he wrote it after mature reflection on the bitter controversy. But as a fact, he wrote it before the public controversy began. He could see it coming, but the papers, as it were, had not got hold of it at the time he wrote. When Arius began to teach his foolish but plausible errors, he found in Athanasius a young adversary of twenty who had already been over just that ground himself, whose dearest principles were the very things he was attacking, who had been living with this very problem and had written down his answer to it. It is really hardly credible, if we did not

[1] It is unfortunate that Athanasius has become associated in the popular mind with the document known as the ' Athanasian Creed '; this document, despite its somewhat quaint language in the Prayer-book translation, is dogmatically unexceptionable if you omit its first two and last two verses. But we had better be quite clear that it has nothing at all to do with Athanasius, nor he with it.

know it as an historic fact, that this polished prose and poised argument is the work of an author so young. But there it is, and to read it makes you think of Athanasius (apart from his subsequent longevity) as the Mozart of the early Fathers.

To take an extract from the *De Incarnatione* is indeed like extracting a few bars from the *Jupiter* Symphony or a few verses from the Book of Job; the sort of operation that should only be entered upon strictly for demonstration purposes. But that said, I wish to quote two extracts. The first is concerned with the humanity of Christ and in particular with his working of miracles. The second concerns his death, its manner and necessity.

De Incarnatione 18

Understand, then, that when the theologians say that Jesus ate and drank, that he was humanly born, they mean that his body, a human body, was born and nourished with the appropriate foods; but they are saying as well that God the Word, who was united with the body, was still ordering all things, and indeed that Christ showed himself, by the things which he did in his human life, to be not man only, but God as well. The body which ate, which was born, which suffered, was his own and not another's; it was the Lord's, and therefore these acts of his are rightly said to be the Lord's acts; at the same time they are acts of a man, because he became man, and it is false to claim that there is in them any kind of pretence: he was truly man. From the human acts of his body he was recognized to be fully present in the body, and equally from the mighty works which he did, using his body as their instrument, he showed himself to be the Son of God (see John 10.37 f.). God is invisible in himself, but he is known through the works of creation; similarly, when he becomes man, he is not seen to be God by any scrutiny of his physical qualities, but it is the works that he performs that proclaim him not merely human, but also the Power and the Word of God. When he reduced the evil spirits to order and drove them away, that was the work of God. Watch him healing the diseases which are the curse of humanity—can you still say that he is man and not God? He healed lepers, he made lame men able to walk, he opened the ears of the deaf and the eyes of the blind: he drove away every disease and every corruption that afflicts men—you could not for a moment miss the finger of God in all these actions. He was able to restore to men faculties that their birth had denied them, as when he gave sight to the man *born* blind; what can this mean but that birth and creation themselves are subject to him, that this is the creator and maker of Creation itself? To give back what birth withheld he must have been Lord of birth. At the very beginning of his earthly life, we must say that he was the maker of his own body—that he fashioned it from the body of the Virgin; he was the maker of that and of everything else: there is no shadow of excuse for mortal minds to overlook the least of the indications of his divinity. The virgin birth itself is proof that he is Lord and maker of all physical things. When the substance of the water at Cana was changed into wine, there was another proof that the

Lord was at work, the Lord and maker of the substance of all waters. When he walked on the sea, revealing his mastery over it, walking on it as though it were solid earth, there is proof of his mastery over all things for those who would discern it. When he fed the great multitude from such a scanty store of food, giving them plenty out of scarcity, feeding five thousand with five loaves and leaving so much over, did not that show that he is the Lord, whose providence is over all his works?

De Incarnatione 21

Now that the Saviour has died for us all, we who believe in Christ no longer lie under the sentence of the law which operated on all who went before. The condemnation has been stayed. The corruption has been arrested and done away by the grace of the Resurrection, so that death now means that we are each released from our mortal bodies at the appointment of God, that we may obtain 'a better resurrection' (Heb. 11.35). We are now like seeds sown in the earth: death is, by the Saviour's grace, not a destruction but a release into new glory (I Cor. 15.53-5).

Somebody may say, of course, 'If it was necessary that he should surrender his body to death on behalf of all mankind, why did he not die privately as men normally do, without going to the length of public execution? Surely it would have been more suitable for him thus honourably to yield up his body than to suffer a death so monstrously ignoble?' But I answer, look again at that argument and you will see that it expresses man's way, but not God's way of working.

What the Saviour did was the act of a divine nature, appropriate to a divine nature. For in the first place, when death overtakes man in the course of nature, it does so because of their natural weakness; they cannot last for ever, and in the course of time their bodies suffer dissolution. Diseases overtake them, and they grow weak and succumb. But there was no weakness in the Lord; he is the Power and the Word of God. He is Life itself. Suppose he had died in private, died in his bed like ordinary men, the obvious conclusion would have been that he died through natural weakness, that he had no more strength than other men. But he was Life, and the Word of God! So see what was bound to happen. This Life and Word must die for all men: but, being Life and Word, he had the strength of life in his body. Therefore, when death must come, he had to borrow the principle and the perfection of corruption from others; it was not in himself; only so could the sacrifice be complete. He who could heal others, could not fall sick; the body that had given strength to others could not waste away. 'Why then did not he prevent his death, as he prevented sickness?' Because it was for this very reason—that he might die—that he had taken a body. To prevent the death would have been to prevent the Resurrection. He hungered indeed, but he did not die of hunger. And furthermore, though he died for the ransom of all men, he did not 'see corruption' (Acts 2.31). He rose in perfect wholeness, for the body was the body of Life itself.

Nobody could call that easy; and yet can you miss the

passionate earnestness and conviction of it? To me the passage where Athanasius so audaciously says that Christ, being Life, had to borrow a technique of dying, is one of the most moving things in Christian literature—the kind of hyperbole that transcends logic and yet clinches an argument.

The two passages are, of course, closely connected, and closely relevant to his central theme. The question before him is: What precisely is the Incarnation and what is its purpose? The answer is to be found in what the Incarnation led to—death, and the Death of death. In his earlier chapters Athanasius sounds a strange and solemn question again and again, like a deep ground-bass—'What was God to do?' He draws a picture of the bedevilment of the world —more than one picture, sketch after sketch, and writes under each one, 'What was God to do?' And then he tells the story of how God 'destroyed death'.

That is the expression he uses; it is hardly necessary to point out that he uses it in the Pauline sense (I Cor. 15.26). There is nothing romantic or unrealistic about him, and you will not think him such a fool as to claim that after the resurrection of Christ there is no death left in the world. 'Death' in that passage means what Paul elsewhere calls the 'sting of death' (I Cor. 15.56); it means not the physical incident of life's extinction, but all the complex of fear, disgust, revulsion and rebellion that has gathered itself round death.

Now observe how he handles the mysterious enigma of the two natures of Christ. Nobody has ever been able to express this mystery in terms of plain logic. A hundred years after Athanasius was writing, the matter of Christ's two natures was still the primary controversy of Christendom. It was argued back and forth for three generations until, in the end, the Council of Chalcedon in 451 put a stop to the official controversy by issuing a declaration in which, in effect, it said, 'This is what Christians have always believed; it is beyond our power to prove it, but anybody who teaches what does not conform to this is an untrustworthy teacher.' But Athanasius in his own day is saying the same thing. Christ is human wholly and divine wholly. No other analysis makes sense of what we know about him. The humanity you could see and touch; the divinity no less unmistakably you could recognize through non-tangible evidences. What you could see was wholly human: what he did proclaimed his divinity.

His handling of the miracles is a good subject for discussion. It might be argued that Athanasius is saying that God made the order of nature, and that God is entitled to modify that order when it pleases him to do so. This is a far from respectable statement. It is not theologically proper to represent God as varying the order of nature simply in his capacity as Almighty, for that is no answer to those who object to miracles as arbitrary interferences with nature's order. Nor does it make the argument any more respectable to say, 'God varies the order of nature according to his will: but that is not capricious variation because God is always good.' For goodness is reasonable, not capricious.

But if we read him carefully, and get the emphases right, we see that that is not what Athanasius is really saying. In all his propositions about the miracles, he is laying the stress all the time on Christ's lordship. And the whole of the rest of the treatise is devoted to the thesis that that lordship is fully expressed in the cross; he exercised and vindicated his lordship, not only over death but over all other things as well, by enduring death and, in the

Athanasian sense, 'destroying' it. The Life had to borrow
a technique of dying—had to place himself to that extent
in humanity's debt. By the same token (Athanasius might
have said), the Lord of creation had to borrow a technique
of submitting to creation, of enduring hunger and thirst
and fatigue, of being liable to human ailments (but not
contracting them, any more than, being tempted, he con-
sented to sin). But the 'signs' not only showed us his
divinity, but were precisely designed to show us his
divinity. Augustine said that the miracles were designed
only 'to lead us to the Father'. The miracles communicate
to us the nature and purpose of God, the Lordship of Christ
over creation. But they are performed in creation by one
who, except his Father permitted him to do otherwise,
underwent the limitations of creation. It is wrong to say
'Jesus healed blind men because he had the power to heal
blind men'; it is better to say 'Jesus healed blind men in
order to show us what kind of power it is that can heal
blind men'; and it is better still to add this, 'He who healed
blind men was he who refused to die in his bed, and refused
to come down from the cross.' Athanasius would readily
agree that all the miracles of Jesus must be seen in the
light of the final and archetypal miracle, the Resurrection,
as leading towards the Resurrection, as preparing us for
the Resurrection. For the purpose of Christ was one and
indivisible and irreversible—to rescue the world from the
corruption symbolized by death and focused in the fear-
fulness and repulsiveness of death. Therefore everything
else he did leads towards that end, prepares us to encounter
that central miracle.

Concerning this question, 'Why had Christ to die?', and
the subordinate question, 'Why must it be by the cross that
Christ died?', Athanasius argues from the essential vitality

of him who could say 'I am the Resurrection and the Life'. It almost looks from his argument towards the end of the second passage as if, had men not laid hands on him, Christ would have lived for ever. What would Athanasius have said if we had approached him with the argument: 'But you say that Christ's work has made of death a cheerful voluntary surrender, a gateway through which a man goes to meet his friend. I agree. But could that not have been done equally well if Christ, when it came to the point of death, had simply made a good Christian end, stripping death of its horror by his example, and showing us how to die?' Athanasius would, I believe, have said, 'There you go! That is what happens when you try to simplify and paraphrase me. You have been misled by that wretched author who has told you that the sting of death is the repulsiveness of death, and you have thought that all that needed doing was the removal of a feeling amongst mortal men about death. But what Christ had to do could not be done merely by setting a good example. What men needed was more than the arousing of right feelings and right thoughts. They needed to be healed of a corruption in themselves. Many before Christ had made a good end. What of Enoch, what of Elijah—men who in Israel's story typified triumphant and friendly death? They did all you are asking Christ to do. No, but in the death of Christ the sin of the world had to be actively and aggressively present. It must appear that Christ was dragged down into death by our sin, by the sin of which you and I are always capable at a moment's notice. Then men could see after-wards the truth of the matter.' After all, in the synoptic Gospels, when he is foretelling his own death Jesus is always reported as saying that 'the Son of man must fall into the hands of men' (Mark 8.31 and parallels). It is only

John, looking back over the events of the life of Jesus from a greater length of time and (surely) a greater height of insight, who could see the truth implied in ' No man taketh my life from me; but I lay it down of myself' (John 10.18). No, it must be death, and it must be a shameful death and a public death, attended with all the degradation and corruption that a man can suffer. And it must be perfect man and perfect God who thus dies. For the good general is he who allows the enemy to deploy all his forces before in one final victorious stroke he surrounds them and takes them captive.

4

AUGUSTINE

On Grace and Free Will

*Augustine, born 354; Bishop of Hippo in North
Africa; died 430. Date of work quoted, 411.*

'It is foolish, generally speaking,' wrote G. K. Chesterton,
'for a philosopher to set fire to another philosopher in
Smithfield market because they do not agree in their theory
of the universe. That was done very frequently in the last
decadence of the Middle Ages, and it failed altogether in its
object. But there is one thing that is infinitely more absurd
and unpractical than burning a man for his philosophy.
That is the habit of saying that his philosophy does not
matter, and this is universally done in the twentieth
century.'[1] That is an adequate exposition of the reason why
'heresy' seems to most modern people an outlandish and
antiquated idea. We are about to meet a heretic now—a
British heretic, what is more: and we must begin by being
quite clear on two points. The first is that heretics always
said things which were very nearly, but not exactly, the
things that most Christians said, and that whenever you
meet a genuine heretic (as distinguished from a merely
slovenly thinker) you are liable not only to find him a sin-
cere and even attractive person, but also to find yourself

[1] G. K. Chesterton, *Heretics*: whichever edition you read, these
words are on the second page of the text.

agreeing with almost everything he says. The second is that he is, in the end, wrong, and his system breaks down under stress.

It is characteristic of the wayward history of the church in Britain, and perhaps of British theology, that the first British theologian of any consequence should be a heretic. His name—or the name by which he was know to Latin Christendom—was Pelagius. I am rather sorry that the pleasant notion that his British name was Morgan has been exploded by the historians.[1] One way and other, during their early centuries, British Christians found themselves again and again out of step with the Catholic church of the Mediterranean. They were told, for example, by Pope Leo in 454 that they were doing things in a manner that would have appeared hopelessly old-fashioned in Rome: keeping Easter on the wrong date, letting the monks adopt a hair-style that had gone out of fashion in Rome a hundred years before, allowing a place in church order for lay people which the more clericalized Roman Christians now found quite inappropriate, and so forth. Much of this happened for the simple geographical reason that Britain was a long way from the centre of things, and that half the notions that were common knowledge in fifth-century Rome were unknown in Britain simply because nobody had come to Britain and insisted on their propagation.

Pelagius flourished at the turn of the fifth century, and in his lifetime there had been a vigorous Christian tradition in Britain for, at any rate, more than 200 years. Tertullian, writing about A.D. 200, mentions it. When St. Augustine of Canterbury was sent by Pope Gregory I to evangelize this

[1] Hugh Williams, *Christianity in Early Britain* (Clarendon Press, 1912), p. 201.

island in 597, he went to preach the Gospel to the bar-
barians who had driven the Britons into Wales and Corn-
wall, and subsequent events indicate that he and his
successors were rightly disconcerted to meet, as they
travelled West, Cadwaladers and Ap-Ifors who said, ' But,
look you, we have been Christians in my family for ten
generations', and who on the strength of that defied the
authority of the new Roman missionary bishops. And there
you have in a nutshell what Englishmen still patronizingly
call ' the Welsh problem'.

The Christian tradition in Britain was vigorous enough
by A.D. 400 to have produced a puritanism; and Pelagius
first appears as a puritan. He is a puritan, that is to say,
in that he becomes conspicuous in his protests against
laxity and disorder in the conduct of his fellow Christians.
He was himself a monk, a lay brother; and he held up to
Christians the ascetic way as an example that they would
do well to follow. He must have been by any standards a
remarkable person, and he must have been operating in a
Christian tradition mature enough to have produced
monasteries and to have produced a situation for a puritan
monk to speak against.

The exact circumstances of his journey to Rome we do
not know; but at the time Rome fell in 410 he had been
there for some years, and shortly afterwards he turns up as
a refugee in North Africa. His preaching and his conversation seem to have made a great impression in Rome. It may
well have been a remarkable thing for the citizens of Rome
to hear the foreign accent of this muscular monk from the
far North, and there was no doubt a rugged naïvety about
the Gospel he preached that appealed to the sophisticated
Roman mind. After all, this was only the second time a
Briton had penetrated near the heart of Catholic civiliza-

tion and left his name in the public records; the first time
was when three bishops went from Britain to a conference
at Arles, and that was nearly a hundred years before (in
314). Reading between the lines both of his own commentary on Romans and of the tracts which Augustine was
subsequently moved to publish in refutation of him, we
find Pelagius to be a highly moralistic, rather unimaginative
person of impressive presence but limited ability in the
finer points of theology. It may be that the secret of his
failure was that while he was magnificent on religion's
moralistic prose, he never came to terms with its theological
poetry.

It was natural that he should read the works of the leading theologian of his time—Augustine, who had been bishop
of Hippo in North Africa since 396, and was when Pelagius
came to Rome a man of about fifty, at the height of his
powers. It seems that in the early days, before they met
face to face, these two had no little regard for each other
through what they had heard and read of each other. But
Pelagius began to frown as he read Augustine, and the
further he read the deeper became the frown. He began to
feel something of what the English liberal of thirty years
ago felt on reading Karl Barth. His spirit was stirred within
him, and in all his sturdy British innocence he lifted up his
voice and protested. The story is told that his decision to
protest was precipitated by hearing it reported that
Augustine had thus summarized Christian morals: *Da quod
iubes et iube quod vis* (a prayer, 'Give what thou com-
mandest, and command what thou wilt'). No doubt he
would have been equally scandalized by Augustine's other
famous epigram, *Ama Deum et fac quod vis* (Do what you
will, so long as you love God). Now Augustine, careful
thinker though he certainly was, was capable also of the

brilliant aphorism, and it is characteristic of a certain kind
a mind that a swift paradox of this sort gives it peculiar
offence. That was Pelagius's reaction to Augustine. But when
he went seriously to work, the British monk's arguments
were strictly theological, and what he contended was
chiefly aimed against Augustine's doctrine of sin. Briefly,
he denied that mankind suffers from an endemic corruption
in consequence of Adam's fall, and he denied that any
supernatural grace is necessary if man is to be healed of
that corruption.

Of course, Augustine dealt very faithfully, in a number
of important tracts, with these contentions, and we shall
have to go into what he said. But first let us admit that
nothing sounds more characteristic of what you would
expect from a British monk than these objections of
Pelagius to Augustine's doctrine. Here was a man whose
whole gospel had been summed up in the phrase 'Pull yourself together'; and the most eminent Christian theologian,
whom good Catholics of his own race knew better than to
question, was saying that the one thing a man can never
do is to pull himself together. Where goes all his sturdy
moralism? How can he go back to his admirers and continue with his campaign of ascetic pep-talking if the Church
is going to say that we are all hell-deserving sinners, and
nothing we can do will alter that state?

I say it was characteristically British, and I do not say
it frivolously. Apart from the common daily experience
which tells us that the average Englishman's religion is still
a belt-tightening, self-pulling-together business, and that
most Englishmen, if they read them, would think Augustine's *Confessions* a shade demonstrative and typical of the
'Latin temperament', consider the comment of *Piers
Plowman* :

I have heard high lords eating at table
Converse as they were clerics upon Christ and his
    majesty,
And lay faults upon the Father who fashioned all men,
And complain against the clergy with crabbed language :
'Why for the works of Adam should we who are living
Rot and be rent? Reason denies it '.[1]

There, in one of that amazing poem's hundred great
character-sketches, is the stout godly English layman.
'Cold bath in the morning and tell the truth : that's been
my way, man and boy. All this parson's stuff about
miserable sinners—they're paid to talk that drivel, I take
it.'

Now Augustine was a bad bishop in many ways, and he
was an impatient and hasty controversialist. But he heard
the poetry of the Faith, and nobody who has not heard the
poetry of the Faith can understand the mystery of sin and
redemption. Augustine made himself as clear as he could
on the matter; but when all was said he could only send
us back to Romans 5, and tell us to read it again as the
word of God. 'As by one man's disobedience many were
made sinners, so by the obedience of one shall many
be made righteous ' (Romans 5.19); that, says Pelagius,
is rubbish, but Augustine says it is the heart of the
Gospel.

But probably the most practical and the most paradoxi-
cal area of the whole controversy is that in which we try
to estimate the place of free will in God's design for his
creatures. Pelagius was very likely a person much given to
talking to people about ' will power'. On the face of it
Augustine's doctrine of Grace seems to leave free will clean

<hr />

[1] *Piers Plowman*, ed. Wells (Sheed & Ward, 1936), I 105-10.

out of the picture. I propose, then, to quote a very famous passage from his *De Spiritu et Littera*[1] which is designed to unravel this perplexity and to re-establish free will in its proper place in God's plan. I choose this work as being the most important and searching of his anti-Pelagian treatises; and we are likely to find that the thoughts that it sets going in the reader's mind are more important than the score it records against Pelagius.

De Spiritu et Littera 52

Does our doctrine of grace abolish free will? That is the last thing we wish to do; on the contrary, we establish it the more firmly by this doctrine. Faith does not abolish the law; no more does grace abolish free will. The law cannot be fulfilled otherwise than by free will; but is not this the true process—that through the law we have knowledge of sin, through faith we are able to pray for grace to overcome sin, through grace we receive healing of our soul from the disease of sin, and through this healing we achieve at last real freedom of the will; then through this spiritual freedom we receive the love of righteousness, and through the love of righteousness the law does the work it was designed to do? The law, I mean, is not abolished, but established through faith, because faith achieves the grace by which the law can be kept; and in the same way, free will is not abolished, but is established by grace because grace heals the will, by which righteousness is voluntarily loved. All these things which I have formed into

[1] *On the Spirit and the Letter*—the title is a reference to II Cor. 3.6.

a chain of spiritual progress are confirmed in the voice of Scripture.

Law says 'Thou shalt not covet' (Ex. 20.17). Faith says, 'Heal my soul, for I have sinned against thee' (Ps. 41.4). Grace says 'Behold thou art made whole; sin no more, lest a worse thing befall thee' (John 5.14). The healed soul says, 'O Lord, my God, I cried unto thee, and thou hast healed me' (Ps. 30.2). Free will says, 'I will freely sacrifice unto thee' (Ps. 54.6). The love of righteousness says, 'The unrighteous have told me tales of pleasure, which are not after thy law' (Ps. 119.85).[1] Well, then, how it is that wretched men dare to boast about free will before their will has ever been made free? How can they boast about their own strength when they are still in chains? Free will means freedom —but they will not hear the real meaning of 'freedom'. Where the Spirit of the Lord is, there is liberty (II Cor. 3.17). If they are the slaves of sin, what free will have they to boast about? 'Of whom a man is overcome, of the same is he brought in bondage' (II Peter 2.19)—you are the slave of your conqueror: how can you be anything else? On the other hand, if they have been set free, why boast as though they had set themselves free? Why boast of what they have received from another, as though it were their own work? Or does freedom to them mean the refusal to acknowledge as Lord him who said 'Without me ye can do nothing' (John 15.5) and 'If the Son shall make you free, ye shall be free indeed' (John 8.36)?

[1] The A.V. reads differently here. Augustine gives a Latin translation of the Greek of the Septuagint.

There is a typically Augustinian passage, a typically Augustinian argument, and if you can see its drift, you can understand Augustine. First we must paraphrase his terms. In the chain of spiritual progress he has six terms: Law, Faith, Grace, Wholeness, Free Will and Love of Righteousness. Let us put his argument in familiar modes of speech.

John Doe is in trouble. He must tell a lie if he is to escape from the consequences of his wrongdoing, and his lie may involve another, an innocent person, in trouble. John Doe hears the *law* in his conscience saying, 'Thou shalt not bear false witness', in other words, 'Lying is wrong'. Now if John Doe's soul is under the protection of the Lord, he will next go down on his knees and say, 'God give me strength to resist this temptation'. That will be an act of *faith*. The act of faith will make him better able to withstand the temptation, because it will have brought into action the *grace* of God. He will now be able to do what before he could not do, because God's grace is working in him. But the consequence of this will be that he 'feels better'; he has got rid of a burden of guilt and anxiety that the lie would have left him with. That is a newly achieved *wholeness* or health of soul. Indeed, he feels more like a free man than he ever did before, and his decision to tell the truth will be a *free* decision. It must be a decision anyhow, but being now helped by God he feels, paradoxically, not that God is moving him about like a chessman, but that he is for the first time acting like a free and responsible person. Then comes the most remarkable thing: he finds that as a matter of fact he wants to tell the truth. He really does *love righteousness*. Not that the consequences of his original action will be any milder because he has told the truth. He may have to go to prison anyhow, but he would say quite truthfully that this, telling the truth, is what he now wants to do, and the temptation to lie was like a bad dream, or like the kind of thing a man would do when he is 'not himself'. He wants what is right. It is right whether he wants it or not, but, miracle of miracles, he wants it, and feels like a man for doing it. And so he finds that the law which said 'Lying is wrong' is a right law. It can be fulfilled now. It is not an oppression. Faith, grace and the rest have made it not a burden but a guide towards the good life. With reasonable application to things spiritual and true, John Doe will be saved even through the application of the law, because he has found the secret of loving the demands of God, not of suspecting them and hating them.

This is the explanation of the astonishing assertion of Augustine that 'the law can only be fulfilled through free will'. It is like him to pack half a page of argument into a sentence, and leave you to work it out: but it does work out.

Now if this is the truth, Pelagius will begin to wish he had never opened his mouth; not because he is defeated in argument, but because he is shown up as having been right about everything but the heart of the Good News. Reversing the old tag, he has won every battle but the last. For what he never saw—and what so many people still do not see—is this crucial point about loving the will of God.

It is always worth while starting a discussion on ethics by saying to somebody present, 'Here are two men. One finds it easy and pleasant to do the right; the other finds it difficult and disagreeable. Both do the right. Which is the better man?' If you hope to begin a discussion you will hope that your friend will answer, 'Why, the second man,' because that is the wrong answer. It may be a good Stoic

answer but it is not a good Christian answer. Christianity
is the only moral system that gives full value to the truth
that God wants us not only to be good but to enjoy being
good; not only to make right choices, but to enjoy making
right choices; and that he does not regard his work as half
done until we admit that we enjoy being good and making
right choices. When you have done some good action, perhaps some costly good action, dare you say, 'But I was
glad to do it'? Dare you sacrifice the moral prestige that
would come your way from the thoughtless if you said 'It
was mighty difficult, and it cost me a lot'? Can you say
that 'But I was glad' without a screwing-up of self-control
and a calculating of other people's reactions? If so you
are where Augustine wants you to be.

Pelagius was almost certainly the kind of person who, if
pressed, would prefer to say, 'The more unpleasant the
duty, the more moral value it has, and the more likely it
is to render you, if you do it, acceptable to God'. Ascetics,
except they be in the first flight (but see chapter 7) are
liable to say that. But it is bad doctrine. God's design is
rather that we should achieve intimacy with him (see
chapter 2) and love what he loves—the true, the honourable,
and the right. Our Lord was not the kind of person who
always regarded his duty as irksome, who made a great
labour of doing the right. He suffered for men's redemption: that is a very different matter. But truly it is written
that 'For the joy that was set before him, he endured the
cross, despising the shame' (Heb. 12.2). If we can hold in
mind these two propositions—that he suffered for men to
the limit of human suffering and dereliction, and that also
he endured the cross 'for the joy that was set before him',
we can apprehend the colossal paradox that lies at the
heart of Christian goodness, and that Augustine is seeking

here to expose. Our Lord's relation with the Father was a
complete blending of his *free* will with the Father's *free*
will, so that what the Father loved, he loved: not so that
what the Father ordered, he carried out.

Pelagius's objection to the total involvement of the
human race in the sin of Adam is, of course, another aspect
of the same problem. Every man, says he, is responsible for
his own sin. Ezekiel agreed with him: but not the apostle
Paul. Pelagius said that we are born innocent: he therefore defied the difficult Catholic doctrine that unbaptized
infants cannot be received into heaven. Most Protestants
nowadays would regard this as one of the points where
they find themselves unable to share Augustine's indigna-
tion against Pelagius. And if we say, as I believe we are
obliged to say, that the sin that shuts men out of heaven
is wilful sin, wilful rejection of forgiveness, then we can
accept Pelagius on the unbaptized infants even though we
do not follow him on the main principle. Paul in Romans 5
speaks of a solidarity in mankind, which in the past had
been to man's loss, and now in Christ is turned to his gain.
This we may interpret as saying that in all humanity, in
all beings that have a free will, there is a gravitation away
from God, an inborn tendency to rebel against God, and
that by the atonement of Christ mankind as a whole is
given the assurance that there is in God nothing that need
cause him this unfounded, unproved suspicion; that God
loves him and cares for him and *respects* him. 'All mankind,' he says, as it were, 'are enemies of God; by grace
God has shown himself friends with them.' Augustine's
point is always that the 'tendency to rebellion' is a consequence of our 'enslavement' to sin. It is an indication
that we are not really free men. If Christ can remove this
pressure that forces us away from God, then we shall again

be free men and, in the words of the old collect, 'stand upright'.

If we do not believe this, what happens? Go back to our friend, John Doe. He made an act of faith. But what reason had he to make that act of faith? Why was it not a blind act of superstitious credulity? Why did he think there was a friendly God waiting to receive him, though he was a sinner? Because he had been shown that it was true. He had evidence. It was true for him, John Doe, not because he was a religious man or a spiritual athlete, but because he was a human being. Not because he had taken a cold bath every morning and told the truth, but because he was a man. If I can believe that, just because I am a member of the human race, the atonement was for me. I must believe that, as a member of the human race, I needed the atonement. There is nothing more sinister than that in the doctrine of Original Sin. Original Sin means only Sin at the Origin, answered by Forgiveness at the Climax.

One other thing this discussion has made clear, as I hope, is the essential connection between good doctrine and the Christian character. It is not to say that all heretics were scoundrels and all the orthodox were saints. I could tell you some stories about Saint Cyril of Alexandria . . . But it does mean that for ordinary folk with no pretensions to great natural goodness, good belief and good works are never very far apart. Ethics without theology makes a barren and profitless study. The ancient Christian beliefs, authenticated, as St Vincent of Lerins said, by 'universality, antiquity and the consent of Christendom' (which includes all the good Christians you and I know) are a very good guide most of the way.

5

CYPRIAN

On the Unity of the Church

Cyprian, born about 200, Bishop of Carthage, died a martyr in the persecution of Valerian, 258. Date of work quoted, 252.

WHEN Archbishop William Temple coined the phrase that the ecumenical movement is 'the great new fact of our time', he summarized a whole chapter of church history in a sentence. But it is an astonishment to many that a movement to draw the churches together towards unity should be a great new fact. Consider what I have just written there: a movement to draw the churches together towards unity. 'The Churches!' We are all so busy applauding the hopeful statements and the really notable achievements of the World Council of Churches that most of us find it difficult to realize just how great an effort a man of the apostolic age would have had to make to perceive any content in the word 'churches'.

We can safely take it that in a real and intelligible sense our Lord founded a church. Dr Bultmann recently said that he did not;[1] but I think that what he meant was that our Lord did not found a sect, a division, a withdrawal from the world. We need not hesitate to believe that Jesus

[1] R. Bultmann, *Primitive Christianity* (English ed., Thames and Hudson, 1956), p. 91.

intended to found, and by his Passion and Resurrection sealed the founding of, a church, a community of the new covenant. He cannot have thought that his Gospel would have prevailed otherwise than through this perfectly natural means. Whatever anybody wants to say about Matt. 16.18, we can accept that.

But when people are shy of believing even this, what they really mean is that Jesus did not found churches. Most assuredly he did not do that. To modern man 'church' denotes so much that is denominational, so much that is of controversy and disunity, so much 'unchurching' of these Christians by those Christians, that his real difficulty is to understand what it was that our Lord did found. And that is where most of us are to-day. We hardly know, without making a large effort of imagination, what 'church' could have meant to the apostles, and they assuredly could not have dreamed of what 'church' means to us. From that generalization I believe we may except the apostle Paul, as we shall see.

Let us begin from there, then: that the word 'churches' is an extraordinary and unnatural development on what the Gospel must have meant by 'church'; that 'church' in the Gospel's sense is a word which has no plural. Then what did that word mean? The word hardly appears in the Gospels—once in Matt. 16 and twice in one verse of Matt. 18, both of which are from the critical point of view slippery passages. But it appears quite often in the Acts. It hardly appears in the Gospels, we must suppose, because in a sense it must have been an idea taken for granted or entirely overlooked by the evangelists. If there was to be any continuity after the departure of Jesus, a community must provide a focus for that continuity. The disciples during the earthly life of Jesus were so intent on believing that these incredible new days would never pass away, that the complexities of the terms which the Kingdom must make with time must have troubled them little. But our Lord was always talking about the Kingdom. He was, moreover, often warning them of what they must expect after he was gone (for example, in John 16). He taught his disciples the way of the Kingdom in such a fashion that after his work was done they could not possibly forget what he had said. The world was not yet the Kingdom. The church, when it came into being, would not be the Kingdom. That he knew. But the verities of the Kingdom were committed to those who covenanted with him from the beginning. More to our present point it is to state that when our Lord conversed with his disciples on the eve of his passion, he spoke much of peace, and of unity, of the work of the Holy Spirit, and of the coming tribulation in which all the sheep would be scattered. He commanded them to abide in him, he prayed that they might be one, he rehearsed, and acted out, his new commandment of love. So St John tells us, and the irresistible conclusion from John's story is that our Lord knew that, whatever their preoccupations at the time, these truths about the Kingdom, and its relation to the community which they must found to provide a continuing embodiment of its principles, were certain to be the greatest problem with which they would be faced after he had gone. This above all they needed to know: this they must be taught with all the solemn urgency that the sacred occasion gave the teaching, that the Church, through the activity of the Holy Spirit, must continue to live in the world, and that there would be a thousand temptations and distractions amongst which it might come to grief if his commandment of love were not obeyed.

What has the notion of 'churches' to do with this? On that we have no direct guidance in the Gospels. In one place our Lord is recorded as saying, 'He that gathereth not with me scattereth' (Luke 11.23), and in another, 'He that is not against us is for us' (Luke 9.50). At one moment he sends his disciples to the outcast of Israel and warns them against evangelizing the Samaritans (Matt. 10.5) and at another he speaks of his sheep that are 'not of this fold' (John 10.16). But behind these superficial and strategical discrepancies in the Gospels there is a ground-bass of unalterable truth, the truth expressed in the New Commandment (John 13.34).

This is where Cyprian can help us: not perhaps in what he says, for what he said in his allocution 'On the Unity of the Catholic Church' he said in a very bad temper; but in giving us the occasion to recall a situation which, though it took place 1,700 years ago, is still in its essentials mournfully familiar.

Here, then, is what Cyprian said in a document which contains one of the most famous—to some, the most notorious—of patristic utterances. This is an extract from the script of the speech he delivered to the convocation of Bishops at Carthage probably early in the year 252.

De Unitate Ecclesiae Catholicae:

passages from paras. 6, 7 and 8

The bride of Christ is chaste and modest; she cannot be made an adulteress. She knows one home, she keeps in uncorrupted chastity the sanctity of one marriage-bed. She keeps us for God, she assigns to the Kingdom the sons she has borne. If any man separates himself from the Church, and consorts with a stranger, he is separated from the promises of Christ, and if he abandons the Church of Christ he need not expect to receive the rewards Christ has promised to the faithful. He is another's possession, he is outside the fold, he is an enemy. The man who will not have the Church for his mother cannot have God for his Father. He can as soon escape outside the Church and be saved as he could have escaped outside the ark of Noah and be saved. Can anybody believe that this unity, which derives from the changelessness of God and coheres in the heavenly mysteries, can be broken in the Church, and torn apart by the force of contending wills?

Who then will be so perverse, so corrupted by treachery, so drunk with the wrath of controversy, that he can believe that the unity of God, the robe of the Lord, the Church of Christ can ever be divided? The words of the Gospel teach us—'There shall be one fold and one shepherd' (John 10.16). Who can imagine that in one place there can be several folds and several shepherds?

There is strong language. What would Cyprian have said of any English village of more than about fifty inhabitants, with its parish church and its dissenting chapel?

Now in order to comment on this we must begin by taking a large view of the whole situation.[1] We may reflect, indeed, at this stage, how it would have gone with the

[1] No better way of taking a large view can be recommended than a reading of S. L. Greenslade's book, *Schism in the Early Church* (S.C.M. Press, 1953).

Church of later days if Islam had not entirely extinguished the Christian Church in North Africa. We are now in our fifth chapter, and every one of the figures we have been discussing had a close connection with North Africa. It needs some effort of imagination to adjust oneself to the picture of a Christian Church encircling the Mediterranean, already established in three continents, when we are nowadays so irretrievably committed to thinking of the Christian Church as existing primarily as a North Atlantic organization, and of Asia and Africa as missionary fields. What would have happened to doctrine, what would have happened to the traditional view of European catholicity, had a medieval African Christendom been allowed to flourish, and had the doctors of Alexandria still been the source of vital Christian teaching?

The situation we are considering took place primarily in Carthage, and the author of these remarkable words was a native olive-skinned African. We do not know when Cyprian was born; his known history begins when he was converted to Christianity somewhere about A.D. 245. He may well have been a man of young middle age—old enough to have become successful as a lawyer, but young enough for his sensational rise to power in the church to cause some embarrassment. We gather that his conversion was a thoroughgoing experience, preceded by a profound sense of the emptiness and frivolity of upper-class life in Carthage as he knew it, and followed by a genuine sense of release and freedom after his baptism. So much he says in his Letters. Within a very short time after his baptism he was a Christian presbyter, and within three years he was a bishop. In those days the First Christian Citizen of Carthage was actually called *papa* (Pope); and we may take it that by this time to be a bishop meant not, as in the first century, simply to be a minister of the Gospel, but that it meant to be a father of ministers, the administrator and leader of a diocese.

It is to be supposed that Cyprian was raised to this high dignity over the heads of many senior and well-respected clergy, and imagination suggests that he must have been a gifted and brilliant person in his own right, since we read that his appointment was no hole-and-corner business, but was genuinely attested by the will of the Christians in Carthage. None the less, there must have been some questions asked in senior common rooms and vestries that day.

Within months of his appointment, persecution descended on Carthage, on the order of a new and highly efficient Roman emperor, Decius (249-51). The effect of this persecution was to face the Church at once with a new and tragic issue. The forty years that went before had been years of peace, and (what is more) years of expansion for the Church. We may take it that now for the first time church members were admitted to the fold who really had not faced the question how much social or political pressure their faith would stand. It was no very new thing for the Church to enjoy freedom from persecution: it is possible greatly to exaggerate the effect of persecution on the Church in these early centuries. But at the same time, the Faith was an 'illicit religion', and the threat of state action was, in previous generations, always there. The new thing in the situation up to the year 249 was that now for the first time on a wide scale profession of faith meant less than 'I undertake if necessary to die for the name of Christ'.

On the recrudescence of state-pressure, then, many

accepted Christians lapsed from this undertaking, or were seen never to have entered into it. That is to say, they did not refuse to make a statutory act of homage to the divine genius of the Emperor. They were required by law to offer to the Emperor, and to the 'genius of the Roman people', a homage that can by a Christian be offered only to Christ. Those who refused were tortured, and frequently put to death; those who capitulated were given a State pardon for their previous offence in being Christians. It was as simple as that. But when the persecution subsided within a fairly short time, on the death of the emperor, the Church had to ask itself for the first time, What is to be done with the people whose faith has not stood up to this crucial test? Are such people to be allowed to call themselves Christians still, to present themselves at the Lord's Table, to receive the benefits of the Church's fellowship and sacraments? Are they to be supposed to be forgiven by Christ in his Church?

The question had to be answered not only in Carthage but also in Rome, and in every other city where the persecution had found out this weakness in the Church's armour. It was the first time the question had arisen so acutely—but not the last time. It became dangerously alive in Germany within recent memory. But it is still a situation foreign to the experience of Englishmen. Suppose, then, that an aggressively godless government gained power in England by popular acclamation, and enacted that every man and woman over eighteen must go to the Labour Exchange and sign a declaration in such words as these: 'I acknowledge the absolute and sovereign authority of the Will of the People. I submit all my judgments, my conscience and my property to that Will, and I acknowledge no other authority whatever. I renounce all other allegiances, and I promise never to obey any other authority than the Will of the People as expressed in the instruments of government.' Failure to sign by a certain date, we will say, means loss of civil rights, confiscation of property, imprisonment in a concentration camp on the Isle of Lundy, and perhaps in the end death. Where would most of us be? What would be the right thing to do?

I need not go further. I shall have to come back to this issue in the next chapter. But all that matters at the moment is to understand that Cyprian, who had taken refuge outside Carthage during the persecution, was quite uncompromising about this. If anybody had repudiated his Christian allegiance through fear of the consequences from the State, he had no hope of being received back into the Church. Those who had capitulated under violent duress might be received back on profession of repentance after a lapse of time.

This was an exceedingly serious thing to say, and it brought a storm round Cyprian's head. As you might expect, there were many who said, 'This is too harsh. It is unrealistic.' Others said, 'But who is this man anyhow? Five years ago nobody had heard of him. It just shows what comes of these risky appointments.' Others again said, 'What does this man know of the ministry and the churches? He had hardly been in the ministry five minutes before they made him bishop.' And finally somebody asked the really damaging question, 'By the way, where is he? I don't remember seeing him much in Carthage.' Public opinion swung round strongly against Cyprian. It was not long before some of his presbyters began to say 'If Cyprian will not receive these poor fellows back into the Church, we will.' And once that was said in one place, it began to be said everywhere. The controversy spread to Rome and to Spain, and there were traces of it wherever the Church had suffered pressure. The opposition to Cyprian in Carthage gathered round one Novatus, while Cyprian was still absent, and he acted swiftly; he circularized the churches demanding that they put an end to their fellowship with Cyprian, and that they apply for the dispensations of all church funds to the new management under the archdeacon Felicissimus. Anybody who wants money, that is, must break with Cyprian.

It was at this point that Cyprian composed his allocution on the Unity of the Catholic Church, from which we took our quotation. We may suppose that he not only published it in writing, but also delivered it orally. And when Cyprian speaks of people dividing the church and causing schism, he is speaking about this situation.[1] The focus of the *De Unitate* is the red-hot personal duel between Cyprian and the men who defied him. The people against whom he uses this passionate language, throwing at them every opprobrious epithet in his fluent barrister's vocabulary, are the rival presbyters, not (at this point) the lapsed Christians. Just before our quotation he had said, 'It is especially our duty, who preside as bishops in the Church, to hold this unity and to witness to it unswervingly, that we may

[1] The rest of the story, which does not concern us here, is that Carthage settled down to a long controversy, which ran parallel to a similar debate in Rome, involving three parties: a 'puritan' party who found the whole business distasteful and advocated separation from a compromised church, led by Novatian in Rome and Maximus in Carthage; the advocates of leniency, led in Carthage by the bishop Fortunatus; and Cyprian himself, of the 'catholic' view. The persecution of Valerian, which began in 258 and in which Cyprian perished, put only a temporary end to the debate, which flared up again at the end of the century and was still, in principle, in action in Augustine's time.

clearly show the episcopate itself to be one and undivided.'
The 'corrupt and treacherous people' who behave as if the
Church could be divided are Novatus and Felicissimus, men
of the ministry who ought to know better.

These are the words of an indignant and wounded man;
his decision to direct the operations of the persecuted
Church from a safe retreat has been thrown in his face as
cowardice; his loyalty to the spirit of Christ has been called
into question, and his authority has been defied.

Now this means, of course, that in one sense Cyprian's
doctrine about the unity of the Church is no more universal
than Paul's about women's hats; that is to say, it is drawn
out of him by the pressure of a local situation. No doubt
when he was composing his treatise he was doing his best
to state universal doctrine, to make himself clear beyond
possibility of misunderstanding; no doubt he was indeed
doing much more than merely 'letting off steam'. But I am
bound to venture the opinion that a good deal of the solemn
argument about Cyprian's doctrine of the Church, based on
these few lines from *De Unitate*, is beside the point. There
have been some who have seized on Cyprian's words about
the unity of the episcopate, hedged about as they are by
copious scriptural quotations, and have said that they prove
beyond doubt that in the third century bishops were part
of the Gospel, and of the essence of the unity of the Church.
Others, approaching Cyprian from the opposite direction,
have held him up as a capital example of a bigoted high
churchman.

But what we read in Cyprian, when we have allowed for
all the rhetoric that the violence of debate has drawn from
him, is that the heart of discord in the Church is always
uncharitableness—always the breach of the New Commandment. There is much in *De Unitate* about the wicked-

ness of separation from the Church, and about the hopelessness of that man's case who separates himself. Every possible scriptural precedent is brought to bear on that argument. But at the climax, in chapter 24, the theme is ' Blessed are the peacemakers '. ' If we are heirs of Christ,' he writes, ' let us abide in the peace of Christ. Sons of God ought to be peacemakers, gentle of heart, honest of speech, bound together in mutual regard, faithfully standing by one another in the bonds of unanimity.' In the end Cyprian's message to the Church is not political at all but simply spiritual.

It is always convenient, but always disastrous in the end, to add to the list of deadly sins an appendix of matters that strike the men of this or that generation as evil or unseemly. Some say that war is a sin; others that the drinking of alcoholic liquor is a sin; in the twentieth century in large areas of society it is a sin to be an intellectual; in the eighteenth century it was almost a sin to be a child. By the same token there are some who say that disunity is a sin. But to talk thus is confusing and inaccurate. There is no need to-day to re-draw the spiritual maps so skilfully and serviceably drawn by the medieval cartographers of the soul, who told us that the deadly sins, from which all other disorders spring, are Pride, Anger, Lust, Covetousness, Envy, Sloth and Greed. Anything else which we are tempted to call a sin can be found to be a consequence of these primary sins. Would the removal of war from the world guarantee the free operation of God's will? Except the sin of malicious anger be removed, the removal of war is nothing more than the removal of controversy. Remove all distinctions of wealth, achieve a classless society, and what have you done, if greed and pride are still as active as ever?

We must ultimately speak in the same way about dis-unity. Disunity may be an unseemly thing; it may be a fearful obstacle to the free course of the Gospel; but it is not in itself a sin. It is not a root but a disagreeable flower. The root is far down in the weed-tangled soil of human nature. To put it concretely, the existence of many Christian denominations in diversity is not in itself sinful; even the regulations of certain churches that exclude members of other churches from their fellowship are not sinful. 'Churches' are not sinful, neither are they virtuous. But here is sin, when one man says of another, 'I have no need of you'; here is sin, when one man says of another, 'I suspect your motives because you seem to be more powerful than I'; here is sin, when a man says, 'I know that the witness of the church is hamstrung by disunity, but I am in no way responsible for it and I shall do nothing to alter it'. Societies and bodies of men cannot sin; only men can consent to sin and connive at the sin of others.

Cyprian says that there is something called 'the unity of God, the garment of the Lord,[1] the 'Church of Christ' which by definition cannot be divided. He says that to suppose that this can be divided is not merely error but nonsense. What is this Church? Obviously it is not the aggregation of all professing Christians, because that *is* divided, and it was divided while Cyprian was speaking; it was divided in Paul's time. It is pietistic nonsense to say of the modern organized aggregate-church that you cannot be in Christ and not in that church. No: but you can with some semblance of sense say that it is impossible to be 'in Christ' and behave as Novatus was behaving—or as Cyprian accused him of behaving. And that is absolutely all that Cyprian can have

[1] A reference to John 19.23-24.

meant. To assent to pride and covetousness and the rest is to fail of our obligation to live as men in Christ; it is to reject the promises of Christ, and the man who lives by those standards need not expect Christ's promised rewards —just as Cyprian said.

Therefore I, being a Protestant, will not accept the charge from a Catholic that I am in sin because I am a Protestant. (To be just, most Catholics that I know do not use that language, and it is not good Catholic doctrine.) But I must listen to him if he says that I prefer the way of pride and covetousness; that I prefer separation to the obligations of fellowship, that I would rather get a reputation for being astutely suspicious ('Ah, but you can't believe all these papists say!') than for being trusting and charitable and large-minded.

Another way of putting what I take Cyprian to be saying is to insist that the ecumenical emphasis of our own day is vapid and unreal except it be allied with a vital evangelical emphasis. I do not here presume to criticize the ecumenical movement; the Inter-Church Aid and Refugee Service of the World Council of Churches is precisely a vitally evangelical work. But we can claim Cyprian's authority for saying that no effort to compose the differences between churches will bear fruit except it be said to each church member, 'Though your sins be as scarlet, I will make you whiter than snow'. For the unity which cannot be divided, that Church from which to separate oneself is to be lost, is the bond of peace, the bond of charity. In charity men share 'the robe of the Lord, the unity of God'. In unity men are one 'even as we are one'. But that unity may come less by devising and planning and searching than by the redemptive miracle which says 'Your sins are forgiven'. Forgiveness is the real bond of peace. That is what cannot be divided. That is the thing from which to separate oneself is to be damned. The sin against the Holy Ghost, in the end, is to say to God, 'I don't want your charity.'

6

CYPRIAN

On Loyalties

I THINK it right to take further in this chapter certain
points which arose in the last, and which we could not
fully deal with there. We were concerned there with unity
in the Church: here we are concerned with the meaning
of Christian loyalty, and with the moral dependence of
men on one another.

We began to discuss there the conduct of the Christian
under state-pressure, the techniques of faith in times of
emergency, but we had to break off what would in that
chapter have become a digression. I want here to put a
point arising out of that on which, as I believe, it would be
useful for discussion to proceed in the Church at the present
time, and which we are in danger just now of overlooking.
I begin from a consideration of the complete disorganization of moral and spiritual values that, except Christians be
extremely vigilant, is bound to accompany a period of
persecution or violence; indeed, any emergency is liable to
produce disorganization.

To take an obvious analogy—we are familiar with the
disorganization of moral values that accompanies war
conditions. For one thing, we are always being told how
much of the corruption of our present society, how much
of the decay of moral fibre among our younger people, is
to be attributed to the Second World War. That is only

one aspect of a highly complicated problem. Nearer the centre of our present discussion is the mysterious problem of heroism and guilt in war time. Who are the good men and who are the bad men in a war? Human nature cannot do without a pattern in the things it contemplates: there must be a good kind of person here and a bad kind of person there, and if we lose our grasp of revealed standards by which we can discern the pattern, we at once set about making patterns of our own and following them—what else can we do? Given that by state decree, accepted by public opinion, it is right to kill and to destroy, is it also right to steal and loot, to commit unrestrained fornication, to bear false witness for the sake of national security? If one commandment is abrogated, how many of the others must go? How far must we 'make allowances' in time of war for misconduct which in time of peace we should unhesitatingly condemn?

Or what is a war-criminal and what is a war-hero? On how many occasions has an act which has won a man a high decoration included subsidiary acts which are by normal moral standards shameful? Let us be fair: public opinion in our country and in others has not been altogether unable to distinguish between the mortal sin that becomes venial in special circumstances and the plain badness which is bad whatever the circumstances. But it is difficult enough and complicated enough. Consider the problems which have beset those who would bring back to peaceful ways youngsters who were committed, for their country's sake, to acts of sabotage and deceit and brigandage in the continental resistance movements. Consider the petty crimes committed by men whose heroism in war-time was admitted and honoured. The pressures of war produce a moral carnage in which truth may be the first, but is not the only casualty. To some extent it will always be true, however objective men think they are able to be, that an act which, performed on behalf of the side which turns out the victor, is honoured, performed on behalf of the other side may be branded as the act of a war-criminal.

In the year 250, Carthage was under a kind of moral martial law that raised questions not unlike these. The only decision that mattered twopence at the time was whether you would or would not submit to the imperial demand to deny Christ. My church, right or wrong, was the slogan: and it was only to be expected that other issues took second place.

Therefore you were left with this situation: that your judgment of a man's final worth depended to a disproportionate extent—perhaps wholly—on one act of his, and on whether that act showed him to be or not to be loyal to his church. More—you allowed yourself to be influenced by his behaviour and his judgments very largely in accordance with his decision on that one point. It was the natural thing to happen. It is difficult for anyone not to be impressed by a man who carries the V.C., and not to treat his views on all subjects as carrying unusual weight. So in the early Church—here is a man who becomes a martyr. The memory of his life becomes sacred and his example is held up as an example to be followed. Here is another who endured a long term of imprisonment. When he is set free he is held in honour, whether or not his subsequent behaviour is honourable. Such a person was known as a 'confessor'.

It is not difficult to imagine the embarrassments to which the Church was subjected in those cases where a 'confessor' turned out to be, in the new limelight of his achievement, a dishonest, arrogant or contentious person. Nor is it difficult to imagine the even keener embarrassment which Cyprian must have felt when he observed that many of the most influential people against him were the very confessors whom he had held up as examples to the Christians who had failed in their loyalty.

It is to this point that Cyprian addresses himself in the middle section of *De Unitate*, and I am putting it here in order to show what prodigious strain was applied to the Church's moral system in these early days, and to display a situation in which moral rectitude demanded of Cyprian that he must say words that appear almost callous in their candour.

De Unitate 21

Confession is the beginning of the way to glory, not itself the title to the crown; it is not the completion of praise, but the beginning of honour. 'He that shall endure to the end, the same shall be saved '—but whatever comes before the end is a step by which the ascent is made towards the summit of salvation; it is not the final step of achievement. He is a confessor—no doubt: but after the confession the danger is greater, because the enemy has been the more seriously challenged. He is a confessor—surely: then it is more urgently his duty to stand with the Lord's Gospel now that he has obtained honour from the Lord through the Gospel. To whom much is given, of the same much is required. It is a serious thing if by a confessor's example another is caused to perish, if from a confessor another learns dishonesty, insolence, treachery. He is a confessor? then let him be humble and modest, controlled in his behaviour, that he who is called a confessor of Christ may imitate the Christ he confesses. He is confessor of Christ—but only if the majesty and honour of Christ are not brought into disrepute through him. The tongue that has confessed Christ must never be given to malice, to violent language, to the shrill controversies of the litigious; above all, never given, after speaking the words of high honour, to throwing poisonous accusations at his brothers, the priests of God. And if a confessor be found after his confession to be living a dishonourable and pernicious life, if he throws away the honour of his confession by sordid living, if he befouls his life with low and detestable actions, if he leaves the Church which made him a confessor and breaks up its unity, exchanging his former faithfulness for treachery, he need not flatter himself that his confession has entitled him already to the rewards of glory; on the contrary, that very confession makes him liable to a far heavier retribution.

We know that we must skim off a certain froth of personal bitterness from this piece of rhetoric; we know why it is that Cyprian makes uncharitable schism the climax of his list of misdemeanours. But on the other hand, if, after that, Cyprian's words sound severe to the point of bigotry to modern ears, we must remember that most modern minds get their moral teaching from the brains-trusts and the press. It is difficult, under stress, to hold the view, but none the less it is only the right view, that ' confession '— a public act testifying to a man's loyalty to Christ in heroic circumstances—does not immediately entitle that man to be heard as an authority on all matters, to be imitated in his conduct, to be dispensed from the normal regulations of a moral society. The artificial prestige of the confessor was a product of the distorted system of values that accompanies the anomalous situation of strife.

But the fact that confessors were among Cyprian's enemies was not the only, nor the worst, problem he had to face. The Christian who had fallen foul of the Church by failing to confess Christ under threats of state action might enlist the help of his friends towards his reinstatement. On the face of it, if a man fell into the state's trap, and confessed allegiance to the emperor, it might be possible to show that he was no more an out and out hypocrite than the confessor was an out and out saint. If he could produce a certificate attesting his loyalty in principle, signed by some persons whom the Church regarded as reliable moral judges, his acquittal from final excommunication might well be achieved. So far nothing can be urged against a humane regulation designed to guard against clerical oppression. But under conditions of persecution, the name of a confessor on a certificate carried more weight than that of the saintliest person who might accidentally have escaped the test. The name of a person who had since died a martyr's death would carry greater weight still. In those conditions, while here and there you would get a genuine case, only too often the confessor was an unreliable judge, or his name might be forged, or his signature might even be bought. Forgeries of martyrs' signatures became a regular religious 'racket' at that time. The confessor, again, might be a noisy, contentious, schismatic person who would sign a certificate without a moment's examination of the case simply in order to make one more gesture against the constituted government of the Church. There was nothing in 'being a confessor' that made any of this impossible. It was all very immoral, and somebody had to say so.

Now every Christian doctrine has its frontier on which constant battle is being engaged against the forces of evil and confusion; and the doctrine that is here in danger of being seriously compromised is that of the Communion of Saints. It is quite clearly a healthy, natural and fortifying doctrine that the stronger may be expected to help the weaker in the Church. You might even say that they cannot help doing so, that they eagerly desire to do so. The example of a real saint in a community is something which the most perverse church order could not suppress if it wanted to; it helps and strengthens the weaker brethren whether they realize it or not. There is a natural sense in which some people seem to have enough goodness to spare some for the common pool, on which their brothers can draw. And if we believe that the incident of physical death is not by any sense a boundary-line of the Church Universal, and that there is any sense in which those on both sides of it are in Communion with each other, then you will freely say that those who have gone before into the eternal world are capable of helping those who are still battling in the temporal age.

So much is, as I hope, sound and commonly accepted Christian doctrine. But a situation such as that in which Cyprian found himself takes us to the disputed frontier. For somehow or other, these certificates of Christian authenticity, bearing the names of confessors and martyrs, were a travesty of the doctrine of the Communion of Saints. Somewhere we have crossed the frontier, and the pattern of values has collapsed. Somewhere prestige has been substituted for holiness.

It is a tragic business, because the faculty of admiration,

the sense of need of one another, is one of the most gracious qualities in the Christian character. Christian thinking takes hold of this natural faculty and need, and makes of it the doctrine of the 'body of Christ'. The devil takes hold of it and makes it the fabric of demagogy and dictatorship and propaganda.

The answer must be that, in the persecution of Decius, the equilibrium of Christian values had been upset by the necessity of the Church's becoming a fighting organization. One artery of the good life had been cut by the Roman tyranny—the artery of justice. Christians were not called to kill men, as Christians are in time of war. But they were called on to do without that security of citizenship, that 'order' in natural political life, which falls within the total scheme of Christian doctrine and behaviour (as is explained in Romans 13), and which is one of the conditions under which a Christian may reasonably hope to carry out his religious profession. That had gone. Therefore Christians must defy the constituted order of society, and this was an emergency suspension of their normal regulations. In the process Christians must expose themselves to the danger of death—another emergency suspension, since in normal conditions it is not a Christian's duty to throw his life away: he must keep it till God asks for it. In consequence a Christian may be called on, by dying, to abandon his wife and children to their fate—yet another emergency suspension, for it is not a Christian's normal duty thus to forgo his natural obligations, and in most normal times it is positively wrong for him to do so even under what he supposes to be a religious compulsion.

It is not uncommonly supposed that the Church is at its best in times of strife and warfare against the secular world. But this is far from the truth. Surrounded by moral earthquake, the adjustments in Christian minds necessary to meet the new emergency-pattern are always imperfectly made, and so it was in Cyprian's case.

When a man has suffered for his faith it seems churlish and unjust to utter sentiments that would lower him in the eyes of his admirers; but the truth must not be hidden for fear of appearing churlish or unjust. In the end it is a question of loyalties. The whole system of loyalties was upset in Cyprian's time, and in consequence loyalties, the loyalty born of admiration, that born of a sense of need, that born of love, were entangled with selfhood, self-preservation, saving of face, even self-advertisement. And I suppose that we can say two things upon this whole matter.

The first is this. We can and must say that to regard sainthood, or the virtue of the confessor, as dependent on achievement, is to go wrong at the start. Cyprian hammers away, not only in *De Unitate* but in everything else that he wrote (especially his Letters), on the conviction that it is not achievement that makes a confessor a worthy confessor. He is, because he has made the loyal gesture, a confessor; but unless he realizes how precarious his position has become, he has not begun to earn a confessor's honour. If he dies for the name of Christ he is a martyr—a witness : but unless he dies in full and charitable communion with the Church, says Cyprian, 'He may be killed, but he will not be crowned'. If he himself rests merely on his achievement, and if others attribute to him special authority on the basis of his achievement, he and they will go into the ditch together. Achievement tells you nothing to the purpose about a man. What matters is what sort of a person he is—whether the achievement is just one part of a picture that is all of the same fine texture, or whether it is an isolated, perhaps even a basely-motived, incident in a thoroughly selfish career, or whether it lies somewhere between the two.

For the vital point is this: though his act may have been a completely good act (and confessing Christ under fear of state pressure cannot be less), can you, can the Church, *trust* the man? How can you tell? In itself the act of confession may not make the man a trustworthy spiritual guide any more than answering the sixty-four dollar question makes a man a wise man, or contributing twenty thousand pounds to a charity makes a man a generous man. How can you tell?

You can only observe, with insight based on the Gospel. Ultimately the question will be whether the man did what he did 'in Christ' or not. 'In Christ' normally means 'in the context of Christ', and there is nothing, however apparently heroic and saintly, that cannot be done from a corrupt motive. There is no single act which, taken by itself and isolated from its context, gives a clear lead towards the answer to the question 'Is this a man in Christ?' The act itself may be good; it may be properly described in all the epithets or eulogy you can find, but except it be supported by a life whose whole habit is humble and gracious, however good it is in itself, it cannot entitle its agent to become a force in the Communion of Saints. In fact, it is never safe to base a judgment about goodness and trustworthiness on achievement. We should base it rather on acceptance. It is what Christ has done for a man, what Christ is accepted by that man as having done for him, that matters.

> The cross is all their splendour,
> The Crucified their praise.

Of some men and women the consensus of the Church is that they lived and walked as friends of the Lord, that their known achievements are part of a homogeneous pattern of humility and acceptance; of others the consensus of the Church is simply that they did good things. A doctrine of the Communion of Saints, though fallibly expressed, is indispensable to a healthy Church, provided we know that we may be rebuked by God in the end both for our admirations and for our condemnations. But if it is 'the Lamb slain from the foundation of the world' who alone is permitted to open the Book of Life and reveal the secrets of life's mysteries, the judgment of the Cross is our best guide. Nothing should diminish our gratitude for every good action we know of. Nothing should dim our admiration for any who give their property, their freedom, their life for their country or their faith. But our gratitude and admiration have nothing to do with the propriety of giving these heroes and martyrs the status of moral authorities in state of Church without such confirmation of their faithfulness as will show that life and death were both of the same heroic and humble stuff.

But secondly, as we walk the Christian way in this life, we do well to remember that to some extent every situation is, in the Cyprianic sense, an emergency; that in every situation there is some pressure, some distortion of values produced by the constant tension with sin. We spoke of what a Christian may be required to do 'in normal times'. But no times are quite normal. There is always a danger of a collapse here or there in our moral system under unexpected stress. There is always a danger that our judgments of loyalty, our acceptance of 'standards', may be made from sentimentality, from haste, from time-serving, from the evil products of anxiety. At any moment the

Christian may be called on to forgo some natural right—the right to security, the right to prosperity, the right to his friends' good opinion—some detail of that kind. At once there will be a reaction somewhere in the faculties of judgment against which an adjustment must be made. Any one of a thousand small matters may upset the equilibrium, and only the Word of God, sought by prayer and fasting, can provide a check by which the equilibrium may be restored. How easy it is for mortal man to lean too heavily on some movement, some popular figure, only to find that they have not the staying-power to bear the weight of men's allegiance! Only Christ has that; and it is well to remember that 'Take up thy cross' is not a command to a single act, but a challenge to a habit of life. Aldous Huxley made one of his characters say of another in a recent book, 'She had been dying by daily instalments. When the final reckoning came, there was practically nothing to pay.'[1] That is what we mean by a homogeneous pattern of life, an equilibrium of temper. It applies not merely to large and spectacular actions, but to all actions and all judgments, and the centre of gravity that determines the equilibrium is on Calvary, the heart and centre of all history and all judgment.

[1] A. Huxley, *The Genius and the Goddess* (Chatto & Windus, 1955), p. 11.

7

BASIL

On Asceticism and the Art of Conversation

*Basil of Caesarea, born 329, Bishop of Caesarea
370, died 379. Date of work quoted, about 361.*

A ND what in the world, you will no doubt ask, has asceticism to do with modern life? Thin and concentrated, monkish and withdrawn, that is asceticism: heroic perhaps in a bread-and-water fashion, but often surely rather 'queer' and uncompanionable. No, asceticism hardly falls under any category that is likely to be useful to contemporary Christians.

Assuming, I trust not unfairly, that this view finds wide currency, I ask for a few minutes' attention to St Basil. I present him not as the founder or inventor of Christian asceticism, but as the man who put it on the rails after its very difficult and unpromising beginning. Basil was the first person to ask the right questions about asceticism, and, broadly speaking, if you want to say rude things about it, they would all have been true if it had not been for Basil.

He was born at Caesarea, a draughty city in the mountains of Turkey, into a wealthy and distinguished family. He was the sort of child who gives his parents plenty of worry about his health, and he was fairly soon sent away to the seaside—the sea being the Black Sea, whose southern shore was, compared with the mountains, a reasonably attractive resort. He had a delicate boy's lonely childhood, and when he went to the university at Athens, after passing through a long educational programme, he was, as it were, a student who pleases his tutors but plays few games. We gather, however, that he was a remarkable talker, and well liked by those who knew that conversation is the best thing that happens at a university. He seems to have made short work of the university course, to have devoured with eagerness everything the lecturers had to offer him, and to have learnt at least as much from his contemporaries as from his seniors. He was first and last a philosopher; and the interesting thing for us is that it was as difficult to be a Christian philosopher in those days as it is now. He soon saw that his life's work was to be the integration of philosophy with Christian doctrine—a thing that was crying out to be done. All round him the Arian controversy (on which see chapter 3) was raging, and nothing, he felt, was more necessary than that there should be some Christians, anyhow, who should recover the faculty of thinking straight, of distinguishing between doctrine and temperament, between disagreement and bad temper.

Therefore Basil conceived the idea of making something of monasticism. He had heard, of course, about the monastic communities that already flourished in Egypt and Syria and elsewhere, and he took two years off to visit as many of them as he could personally. What he found almost certainly confirmed the ideas with which he had started out, namely, that this was not, in its present form, of much use to anybody, but that it was a principle which could be reapplied with enormous benefit to the Church.

His 'working life', therefore, consisted of two parts— parts not historically separate but quite clearly distinguished. One part was the organizing of a large monastery in his favourite place at the seaside, near where he had spent his youth: the other part was playing the role that a man of his family and gifts was called on to play—first assisting the Bishop of Caesarea in administering the diocese, and then, on the Bishop's death, succeeding him. It may broadly be said that the monastic part was what he loved, and that the rest he performed with great reluctance and only at the urgent request of his family. In both capacities he found himself engaged in theological controversies, but these he found, on the whole, more distasteful than everything else. What we are here interested in is his conception of the ascetic life, and I shall first offer an abridgment and paraphrase of part of his Second Letter, written to his friend Gregory, who became Bishop of Nazianzus. Then we will comment on it.

From Letter 2

We try to keep our minds at peace. An eye which is always gazing here and there, left and right, up and down, can never see clearly what lies before it, and it is the same with the mind. I mean that, for example, in the world an unmarried man is always being upset by unruly desires, and a married man exchanges these for a host of other worries. If he has no children he hankers after them, while if he has them they cause him a lifetime of anxiety—all this added to the hurly-burly of the world's business. What can one do, but separate oneself from the world? But do not misunderstand me. Withdrawal from the world is not a physical removal from it; it is the separation of the soul from bondage to the body. This involves leaving one's home, possessions, friends and all the rest: but it brings with it the capacity to receive in the heart the impressions placed there by God's own instruction. This means unlearning a good deal of teaching that may be already there; you can't write on wax without first erasing what has previously been written on it. Solitude helps here, because it calms the passions and gives an opportunity to reason to release the soul from dependence on them.

The beginning of the soul's purgation is tranquillity —where the tongue takes a rest from gossip and the eye from licentiousness and the ear from buffoonery (this last I particularly welcome!). Thus set free, the mind can become occupied with the cultivation of all the virtues, and with the thought of the glory of God.

The study of the Bible is the best guide to the discerning of one's duty. What with moral precept and the example of good men so abundantly set forth there, you have all you want. What better encouragement to chastity is there than the story of Joseph? Where will you learn humility better than from Job? or courage, better than from David? Or the true Christian mind— courage together with humility—where is that better set forth than in Moses?

Such reading always moves you to prayer. Prayer has this priceless reward, that it forms in you a distinct idea of God. We ought to cultivate the high felicity of becoming temples of God—God always living in us. There is no better weapon against the disturbances of passion than that.

From this proceed all sorts of details of practice. We prefer to be careful to avoid frivolity in conversation, to learn to ask questions without contentiousness, to answer without self-display. We should not interrupt the speaker when he is saying something profitable, nor be eager to throw in our own words in order to appear clever. We should neither be too proud to learn nor too impatient to teach. We should take care, when we have learned something from someone else, not to pass off the idea as our own, but to give the credit where it is due. In conversation it is best to use a moderate tone of voice, neither mumbling nor shouting. Think first, speak second. Be affable and agreeable in all conversation; smart wisecracks are a poor way of gaining popularity; we should depend on a gracious habit. In rebuke we try to avoid roughness and to do all in the context of Christian humility.

We tend to express this abasement of ourselves in a somewhat grave demeanour. If our eye is downcast, our outward appearance unkempt and our clothes often in need of cleaning or patching, it is not, as it would be in secular life, an affectation of public mourning. It is because our minds are on these inner things. We are in our way particular about dress. We keep our tunic in place with a girdle, but we do not wear this so high that we look dandified, nor so loose as to look like tramps. When we walk, we seek to express neither sluggishness in lounging, nor brashness in hurrying. We are not interested in brightly coloured clothing, but only a fool would come and live out here in anything but good, thick wool. We eat what is good for us, bread and vegetables, and we drink water. Anxious gluttony is, of course, quite out of place. We do not neglect to think of God as we eat, preferring to make the food itself an occasion for glorifying him. Before meals we remember in prayer God's promises; after them, we give thanks.

Heavy sleep is not our habit: our diet makes it unnecessary anyhow. Our kind of light sleep is also much more refreshing. Midnight is our cock-crow; midnight is a grand time for quiet recollection of the glory of God, and for invoking his help against all the things a man has to contend with.

I do not think I need apologize for the colloquial character of this paraphrase. It is written by a man of 30 to a close friend, on the subject nearest his heart. Basil was a first-class letter writer, having that gift, rare in all ages, of making you feel through his letter that he was speaking to you. As a matter of fact, good letter-writing is one of the first consequences of the kind of life to which he is introducing us.

Now what Basil is writing about is his vision of a monastic community, and it was the organization of a large monastic society that was Basil's most notable contribution to Christendom. But up to now monasticism had been an odd and precarious business, rightly looked on with suspicion by many reasonable Christians, and we must for a moment look at its earlier history.

The principle of large-scale withdrawal from normal civilized life first appeared on an impressive scale in the Montanist movement in the later second century. Mon-

tanism was a quasi-puritan movement in which men and women indulged in ecstatic prophecy, believing that it was their duty to found a community in Phrygia (Southern Russia) which should be a special vessel of the Holy Spirit. There was much talk of the imminence of a new dispensation of God, a reign of the Holy Spirit, which would afford primary authority to members of the movement. Withdrawal implied a renunciation of the ties of the world, including marriage, a system of fasting, and a relinquishing of all conventional forms of church organization and of state loyalty. The eminent theologian Tertullian was a member of this movement.

This was an early example of the founding of a community of Christians within the Church; but it was a false start because so much of 'the Church' was denied or laid under criticism by it. Indeed, Montanism is usually regarded as a heresy, and its primary purpose was not to enrich the Church but to withdraw from it as well as from the world. The true monastic tradition probably began with the eremites of the Nile—but among them at the beginning there was little sense of community. Their most conspicuous leader was St Antony, whom Athanasius knew and whose biography he wrote. At the beginning the eremites (or hermits) of the Nile were men who lived by themselves, cultivating a solitary religious life and living on the barest necessities. Many of them became as it were popular oracles for the people who lived round about them, and built up small practices in a primitive form of what the Americans now call 'counseling'. But their religion was entirely untheological; indeed to a large extent it was superstitious. The people's habit of consulting them gave them a certain fluency in their practice of the confessor's art, but anybody like Basil could see that most of the time they hardly knew what they were talking about. The literature that emerges from this culture indicates a disconcerting tangle of folk-lore and ghost-lore, and historians like Lietzmann and Harnack manage to include a few sordid details in their accounts of the movement. We cannot rehearse them, and this is no place for gossip, but the gospel according to the Egyptian monks was often grim, fear-ridden and spectral. They were in the wilderness and they were indeed 'with the wild beasts' of fear and superstition which form the grimmest aspect of the really solitary life.

Their greatest organizer was one Pachomius, a man who came to Christian monasticism from the army, and who, with characteristic military energy, set about re-casting the solitary hermitages into small groups. In consequence their solitude was to some extent mitigated. But revolutionary though the work of Pachomius must have been in its denial of the necessity of complete solitude, it did not answer the real question, which was, Where were monastics to find the spiritual and intellectual counterpoint that would stiffen their resistance to the religious and psychological temptations of their way of life? Pachomius, good man though he was, could not deal with that.

There are other sides, of course, to this story. Syria and Asia Minor have a better record. What was going on east of Palestine we know next to nothing about. But if the reader will supply the common knowledge which any Christian will have concerning the witness which the ascetics attempted in principle, and will then add the notions to which these paragraphs have given expression, together with the perfectly historical but very puzzling stories of people like Simeon Stylites, who served the Lord by sitting on a pillar for forty years, he will have a fair idea of the scene on which Basil entered.

Those who want the details of Basil's idea of how a a monastery should be run can extract them from Basil's two sets of Rules, known as the Longer and the Shorter Rules. These are far from systematic, and Dr Lowther Clarke[1] tells us that they are transcripts of answers given by Basil to questions at conferences to which he was called by people who were in need of guidance. These show that no detail was too trivial for Basil's attention towards the perfecting of ascetic practice. But the question now must be, What precisely is asceticism?

'Ascetic' derives from a Greek word, *askesis*, which means 'exercise' directed towards some specific end: what we should call 'training'. It is the five hours a day required of the concert pianist, the consistently maintained discipline of the Olympic runner. The word is very common is classical Greek, but it appears only once in the New Testament, where the author of First Timothy writes 'Bodily exercise profits for a season; but the godly habit is profitable always, since it gives you a hold on the promises both for this life and for the life to come.'[2] The letter-writer is distinguishing *askesis* (bodily exercise) from *eusebeia* (a godly habit). I fancy that the notion of *askesis*, of discipline in terms of giving up things in this world for the sake of achieving a godly habit, is not one to which any New Testament writer gives much prominence. The nearest Paul comes to it is, of course, the passage about running the Christian race in I Cor. 9. But the true New Testament basis of asceticism is taken as far as it can be taken—in my judgment perhaps a little farther—in the

[1] W. K. Lowther Clarke, *The Ascetic Works of St Basil* (S.P.C.K., 1925), p. 17.
[2] A fresh translation, embodying my conjecture as to the true meaning of the words translated in A.V., 'profiteth little' (I Tim. 4.8).

first chapter of that very interesting recent book, *Christian Asceticism and the Modern Man*.[1] The notion of systematic discipline in this life is Greek rather than Biblical. The letters of Paul, especially in their practical passages, are so strictly occasional that if we take his advice in matters of worldly discipline as being of universal application we shall fall into the old and rusty trap of thinking that the Bible condemns marriage because of what is written in I Cor. 7. The New Testament is so vitally concerned with the exposition of that New Life to which asceticism is only one of many preliminary exercises that it was precisely possible for enthusiastic Christians, such as the pre-Basilian monks, to lay too much stress on the end, and too little on the means, with the result that they became prematurely airborne in their doctrine and therefore unsafe against superstition and temperament.

No: asceticism of the Basilian kind is a Greek philosophical notion, and it is the best thing that Greek philosophy gave Christendom. It derives, as you will see if you glance again at the beginning of our extract from Basil's second letter, from the venerable idea of *theoria*, of 'seeing what is really there', which was a preoccupation of the Greek mind. Whether it be Platonism proper, or Stoicism, or any other respectable Greek system, the *summum bonum* is the withdrawal from distractions in order that a man may come to knowledge, or intimacy with the truth. Basil's notion of asceticism is the development of a Christian technique which, by canalizing a man's energy, should leave him free to become intimate with God.

This Christianizing of Greek philosophy was a hazardous

[1] *Christian Asceticism and Modern Man*, essays by various authors (Blackfriars Publications, London, 1955).

business, as we have seen already (chapter 2). The collision between the idealism, the essential withdrawal, the tendency to aristocracy in Greek thought, and the Gospel of the Word made Flesh was a head-on collision. But Basil's solution is persuasive. Everybody since Pentecost had said that a Christian must act rightly. Basil adds that he must think rightly, too. Right thinking demands discipline. This he had been taught by his university masters, and it was a happy accident that the fashionable way of thinking and conversing at the university was, in his time, a way (called technically the 'Second Sophistic') particularly attentive to clarity of style and precision in the use of words. It was this, by the way, that made him such a good letter-writer. He had been brought up to value exactness above rhetoric, to exert self-control in his thought and speech, and the moral equivalent is summed up in the favourite word of his monastic movement—*enkrateia*, 'mastery of what lies within'. To the pagan philosopher this 'self-mastery' had the purpose of promoting exact knowledge; to pagan religion it promoted mystical unity with the Infinite; to Basil it promoted intimacy with God in Christ—and there is your Christian translation of Greek philosophy.

You may say that this is all very well for monks; but monks are by the nature of their trade withdrawn from the world. What use is it to people who live in the world? The answer is twofold. In the first place we can say historically that the idea of the Basilian community of contemplation was not merely to place the monk individually nearer to God, but redemptively to draw the world nearer to God by example, precept and the practical fruits of contemplation. One of the most obvious ways in which this was actually done was in the writings and sermons and hymns of Gregory of Nyssa and Gregory Nazianzen,[1] two close colleagues of Basil, whose writings did more than the writings of any of their contemporaries to keep theology on an even keel during the turbulent years between A.D. 300 and 400. Another obvious fruit was the amount of charitable work that was done by the monks and nuns in their districts, to which abundant references will be found in the other letters of Basil.

But, secondly, common experience witnesses to the universal necessity of what Basil was saying. Consider the paragraph of his letter which refers to conversation. How many people can carry on a fruitful and steady-going conversation, even *à deux* in the company of an intimate? How many have any technique of continuous discussion in a group of people? How many, in common speech, can distinguish between what is central and what is tangential? How many can write in a letter precisely what they mean? Let conversation be a parable of the whole, and we must see at once that the secret of good conversation is *askesis*, mental and temperamental discipline. The enemies of good conversation are disorderly thinking and disorderly feeling. Here is a man who mumbles his words and falls over himself, who cannot speak two sentences with clarity and authority. Here is another who will never let you finish what you are saying. Here is a third who never listens to what you have said, but goes on from where he left off as though you had not spoken. It is not only lack of mental discipline that causes these common faults; it is lack of emotional stability as well. There are moments of fear, distrust, suspicion, self-justification which throw the whole

---

[1] For an accessible hymn by Gregory Nazianzen, translated into English, see no. 431 in *Congregational Praise*, 458 in the *Church Hymnary*.

machinery out of gear before it has been running two minutes. If you told a stammerer that he might well be cured if he could be persuaded to control his body in an efficient fashion, to stand, walk, and sit down with disciplined movements instead of with nervous, shambling, jerky movements, he might be surprised; but in effect that is what Basil, with his integration of physical, mental and temperamental discipline, would say to him. (Curiously enough it is precisely what he would be told at the F. M. Alexander Institute in Westminster, whose record of cures of all manner of intractable mental and emotional conditions through simple physical disciplines is exceedingly impressive). But whatever it is that makes language so effective a concealer of our thoughts, its removal depends on an habitual discipline. Good conversation demands a machinery for communication which acts smoothly and effectively at once, not one that has to be cranked up each time for action. Listen to this, from a later chapter of *Christian Asceticism and Modern Man*, on the man of disciplined habit:

He may be taking part in a tennis tournament and finding himself in the grip of a formidable opponent, or he may be at the wheel of a car and suddenly have to negotiate a dangerous corner. In both cases he will promptly and with ease take whatever action the situation requires, even though this may be the first time it has been demanded of him.[1]

Conversation is always a series of unprecedented emergencies, which is why it makes so adequate a parable

[1] Op. cit., pp. 241 f.

of life as a whole. We seem to have here part of the answer to the problem of the continuing emergency which we put in the last chapter. The ascetic habit is designed towards this end. There is all the difference in the world between this and a blind following of tradition or of instructions. That gives you the person who can do excellently everything he has been shown how to do, but who is floored by every fresh demand. Asceticism in the Christian context has the aim of setting the mind free to follow and obey the Word of God that is new every morning.

As the book I have quoted suggests, modern life is chiefly impeded not by physical distresses but by men's inability 'to cope with overwrought feelings and satisfy the need they feel for a less superficial existence'.[1] Bodily deprivations probably should play a smaller part in modern asceticism than they played in Basil's scheme, because our chief enemies to peace and good order are not biological but psychological. What modern man has to deal with is the attitude, for example, among some folk towards the cinema that causes them, if they miss a week's visit, to feel almost that they have failed to propitiate a deity. The world's chief temptations come in the form of idolatries and addictions, and to-day's worst temptations are mental and psychological addictions. The answer is in a new asceticism, a new mastery (not suppression) of 'what lies within'. We need a modern translation of the medieval 'contempt of the world' that does not use the word 'contempt', a word of somewhat soiled meaning nowadays, but rather such a word as 'good-humoured encounter'. The modern ascetic is not so much the man who chastises the world with contemptuous wrath, but rather the man who, because he takes Christ so seriously, simply cannot bring

[1] Op. cit., p. 259.

himself to take 'the world' very seriously. He is neither in love with it nor afraid of it, because he has allowed God to train him to see 'what is really there'.

By an historical accident asceticism seems to be identified with celibacy and monasticism and regular worship at odd hours of the night. These are accidents of it, not properties of it. By a large historical misunderstanding it is associated by some with the repression of the spiritually submissive by the spiritually unscrupulous, those 'wicked abbots'. The truth is that this 'mastery of what lies within' is the way for men to resist the small and the great tyrannies that bedevil modern civilization. What, after all, can Big Brother do against a man of truly ascetic mind and heart?

8

JOHN OF DAMASCUS

On Visual Aids

*John Mansur, Monk of Damascus, born about 695,
died about 750. Dates of works quoted, 726-736.*

JOHN OF DAMASCUS, often known as the last of the
Fathers, was born and flourished about three centuries
later than the last of the other figures in these discussions;
and it may seem a strange thing to bring him, from his
medieval remoteness, into a circle which is otherwise tidily
rounded off by the fifth century. But I am doing so
because he was very loquacious, in three Orations ' Concerning those who Reject Images' at an early stage in the
Iconoclastic controversy, and I trust that this chapter will
show why the issues he raises deserve the careful thought
of modern Christians.

John is best known to modern churchgoers as the author
of the Greek originals of two well-known Easter hymns,[1]
and that would not have displeased him, for he would have
wished to be remembered as a leader in the great artistic
tradition of Byzantine Christianity. The controversy in
which he was involved, on the question whether visible
images representing our Lord and the saints were permis-
sible in Christian churches, afforded him the opportunity

[1] ' Come, ye faithful, raise the strain ' and ' The Day of Resurrection '; 140 and 141 in *Congregational Praise*, 131 and 137 in the
English Hymnal.

of making some comments on the theology of aesthetics which are worth our attention. To-day we are not liable to become heated over the question of pictures and statues in church, for that is a question over which Christians of different traditions seem happy to agree to differ; but if for 'images' we substitute 'visual aids', we find ourselves in the middle of a subject which, though perhaps not as controversial as it ought to be, is one on which the modern church is becoming very active.

The Iconoclastic controversy ('iconoclasm' means 'breaking down images') was a protracted business, less than half of which could possibly be called theological. Many currents of hostility and suspicion assimilated themselves to the controversy, and by the end of it the Eastern half of Christendom, usually called 'Byzantine' or 'Eastern Orthodox', had broken off relations with the Western half, now usually simply called 'Roman Catholic'. The controversy began with the edicts against images of Leo III in 725, and closed with the Decree of Restoration by the Empress-regent Theodora in 842. At the beginning of the controversy Byzantium (now Istanbul) was still the centre of the imperial government of the 'Roman' empire; but ever since the time of Justinian (emperor, 527-565) there had been tension between that imperial government and the Roman papacy. Indeed, the cleavage between the Eastern and Western cultures in Christendom went deeper than that. Back in the time of the Arian troubles you can see how many of the Arian supporters came from the East and how jealously orthodoxy was guarded in the West; and how characteristically the emperors, once Byzantium became the capital of the eastern half of the empire on its re-foundation by Constantine in 324, hardly knew which side they had better support. Perhaps it was fated from the beginning that the Eastern Christians should say 'Christianity was born in our half; you Romans must respect our apprehensions and instincts in Christian interpretations' while the Westerns said, 'We make the laws and run the empire, and make the world safe for you; so do not imagine that you can reckon without us.' The final breach did not come until the year 1054, but in John of Damascus's day there was little love lost theologically between the two halves of Christendom.

But neither is the issue about visual representations of divine and sacred persons in church a new issue. It is discussed at various points in the earlier Fathers, and to read most of what they say one is surprised that in the end the Church decided, as it did decide, in favour of their retention. The reasons for that, to be sure, were partly political and historical. Had Christendom been in the early Middle ages a Latin church simply, images would almost certainly have gone.

John of Damascus is not, of course, interested in the political aspects of the discussion. He has certain theological arguments to bring forward in favour of these 'visual aids', and wherever you pick up his three treatises you are likely to encounter them. The treatises are to the modern eye wearisomely repetitive, and filled out with plenty of uncritical and allegorical reference to the Old Testament. But modern Christians, and especially the iconoclastic type of Protestant, may well turn again to these old arguments in favour of images, and see what corresponds to them in the modern scene.

Most of my readers, actually, are likely to be of an iconoclastic turn when it comes to church ornaments. The whole of English nonconformity is virtually iconoclastic, and so is a good deal of opinion in the Church of England.

The presence of images and pictures in church is still heavily resented by the 'old guard' on grounds that have little to do with aesthetics. And the iconoclasts begin with a very weighty authority on their side—the Old Testament itself, with its commandment, 'Thou shalt not make unto thyself any graven image.' True, the commandment further forbids the worshipping of graven images, and everything really depends on whether you interpret the commandment as saying 'You may make an image but you must not worship it', or whether you think it says 'You must not make an image because if you do you will be unable to help worshipping it'. The Old Testament mind in practice took the second interpretation. Images themselves, not merely the worship of them, were forbidden. Moreover Islam, that most formidable enemy of Christianity in the eighth century, took exactly the same line. Therefore Jewish converts to Christianity, and those converted from Islam or from pagan cultures devoted to idolatry, formed a large section of public opinion against any kind of visual representation in church. By contrast with that very lively conviction, most modern iconoclasm (excepting always that of Cromwell's army) is conventional rather than convinced; but, if it becomes a controversy, the Old Testament is brought in as the first witness against images and pictures. If Christians wish to defend them, what they really have to do is to prove that the New Covenant has revised this part of the law of the Old Covenant. And we shall have to see what the New Covenant has to say by way of guiding and restraining us in our use of new-found techniques of visual aid.

Now John's arguments, which in a moment we shall rehearse in extracts from one of his treatises, amount to these:

First: if you will not make an image of Christ, your Christology is faulty.

Second: the objection is gnostical, because it implies a derogation of the material world.

Third: if you reject images, why admit books?

Adversus eos qui imagines abiciunt 2:

extracts from paras. 9, 11 and 13

(9) When we set up an image of Christ in any place, we appeal to the senses; and indeed we sanctify the sense of sight, which is the highest among the perceptive senses, just as by sacred speech we sanctify the sense of hearing. An image is, after all, a reminder; it is to the illiterate what a book is to the literate, and what the word is to the hearing, the image is to the sight. All this is the approach through the senses: but it is with the mind that we lay hold on the image. We remember that God ordered that a vessel be made from wood that would not rot, gilded inside and out, and that the tables of the law should be placed in it and the staff and the golden vessel containing the manna—all this for a reminder of what had taken place, and a foreshadowing of what was to come. What was this but a visual image, more compelling than any sermon? And this sacred thing was not placed in some obscure corner of the tabernacle; it was displayed in full view of the people, so that whenever they looked at it they would give honour and worship to the God who had through its contents made known his design to them. They were not worshipping the things themselves, of course; they were being led through them to recall the wonderful

works of God, and to adore him whose words they had witnessed.

Or you will recall that God commanded that twelve stones be taken from the bed of the Jordan, to this end (Josh. 4.21) that 'When your children shall ask their fathers in time to come, saying, What mean these stones? then ye shall let your children know, saying, Israel came over this Jordan on dry land.' Then why should we not make representations of the precious sufferings of Christ the Lord? We make them so that when my son asks me, I may say, 'God the Word was made man, and through him not merely did Israel pass over Jordan, but all nature was restored to its original felicity. Through him our human nature was raised from the lowest depths of the earth, above all earthly powers, to sit on the very throne of God.'

(11) No, it is forbidden to make an image of that Divinity which has nothing to do with the material, is without body and invisible, without shape or colour. And anything fashioned towards the worship of the devil or of evil spirits should go to the flames. Anybody who makes an image of a man, or a bird or a reptile, or any other created thing and treats it as though it were God, falls under anathema. But the contempt of the material because it is material is a Manichean error. Scripture testifies against the forbidding of the use of material things as a help to the worship of God. (13) Flesh is material—can you deny it? My salvation was brought to me by material means. and I venerate the wood of the blessed Cross, not as though it were

God, but as being full of the work and the grace of God. The hill, Calvary, the tomb, the stone, the very source of the Resurrection—all are material; the ink and the pages of the Gospels, the table from which we take of our salvation and all its furniture, the very body and blood of the Lord—all are material. You must either forbid all respect to these things, or you must allow with it respect to the images consecrated to the name of Christ and to his friends, the saints, as being over-shadowed by the grace of the Holy Spirit.

Having heard John of Damascus arguing that images are a reminder of the goodness of God, and that to despise the material is to fall into an ancient error, let us now return to the Scriptures and see whether we can discern the word of the New Covenant on this matter.

Initially we may say that the Mosaic prohibition on graven images may well have had much to do with the fact that all the neighbouring tribes worshipped idols, and that by denying themselves any kind of images the Jews were able to emphasize the distinctiveness of their religious witness. But is is clean contrary to the character of the Mosaic law to base so vital a part of its teaching on the mere fact that it is necessary for Israelites to behave differently from their neighbours. We expect it to say quite bluntly that they must behave better than their neighbours, and therefore to imply that worship without images is higher and truer than worship with them.

Now the Old Testament is equally clear on two great religious points. One is that no man can see God and live, the other is that no man can hear the Word of God and die. The exceptions to the first principle (Ex. 24.11, Isa. 6.1 and

Job 42 are the best known) are rare, though important. Exceptions to the second do not exist: 'If thou be silent unto me, I shall be like unto those that go down into the pit' (Ps. 28.1). There is an underlying assumption that while sight is liable to mislead, in respect of hearing men should be urged to unstop their ears. All this is a generalization that close Old Testament study would need to modify. On the one hand, men were urged to 'behold the works of God', on the other they might not pronounce the ineffable Name. But we may still note that the prohibition of images lies side by side with a richness of verbal imagery in description of the character of God unequalled in any other religious literature.

Now it is more than probable that the prominence that the New Testament gives to the miracles of our Lord in which blind men are given sight is a symbolic prominence. There can be no question that it is so in the Fourth Gospel. In John 9 we have the dramatic counterpoint of the two kinds of blindness, the innocent and curable blindness of the blind man, and the disastrous spiritual blindness of the Pharisees. The 'sign' within the 'miracle' is surely the power of Jesus not only to grant physical sight to the unsighted, but to grant *vision* to those who have eyes but cannot see: with the solemn addition that, before that final miracle can be performed, he must die and rise again.

This is where John the Evangelist amplifies John of Damascus for us. For he urges us to ask 'To what end is the giving of sight designed?', and therefore, 'To what end do we design visual aids?' Now John of Damascus said that visual aids were appropriate to the illiterate—and there he exposed a great moral danger in our use of them. People who cannot read can understand pictures. People who do not want to read can be persuaded by pictures.

People who are too lazy and uncritical to read can be
brought into line by pictures. Big Brother can do with television ten times what Dr Goebbels did with radio. Exactly;
once we think of visual aids as an aid to *instruction* we
are wrestling with the power of the educator, the power
of the strong mind over the weak or growing mind. And to
all educators the Church must say with quite unmistakable
emphasis that the only kind of religious education that
matters two straws is that which leads to this end: 'And
their eyes were opened, and they knew him.' Visual aids
must be aids not towards sight but towards vision.

We may say that a man cannot know Christ if he himself is less than a man; if what passes for a 'visual aid'
atrophies his critical faculty and encourages him to rely
on impression and feeling and to leave his reason out of
his religious life, it is reducing him from his manhood and
acting on him like a drug. This is the great danger in the
argument that visual images are appropriate to the illiterate.

I fancy that these convictions are partly confirmed by
what is a common opinion about the use of television in
modern society. It is, I think, a fairly widely accepted
opinion, though not always a carefully analysed or carefully expressed opinion, among moralists that television
can be a menace. It is not to the present purpose to argue
that television at present provides a lower standard of
entertainment than radio. The burden of the moral argument that television should be treated by the Christian
with an almost ascetic caution is that television by its
special techniques can make the viewer more receptive to
falsehood by simply encouraging him to lie back and
extinguish his critical faculties. There is no inherent reason
why it should do so; but many believe that as a matter of
fact it does do so. They believe it, I fancy, for much the

same reason at bottom that made the Israelites hew down the idols.

Moreover, there is much truth in the well-known line of the hymn, paraphrasing I Cor. 13 (but at this point actually adding to it) which runs, 'Faith will vanish into sight'. You can place a double meaning on that. Taken one way it means that, in the eternal world, what is now accepted by faith will be received fully and in reality. 'Faith,' as it were, 'will vanish into vision.' Taken the other way it could mean that sight extinguishes faith. And that suddenly becomes a very relevant observation if we recall Dr Micklem's classic comment on Hebrews 11 that in that chapter 'faith' means among other things, 'imagination'.[1] Where shall we be, where will our religion be, if no room is left in it for imagination? Was it not in fact the most positively humane, we might even say the most evangelical, note in that ancient commandment against images, that the removal of images left room for imagination and faith in lives from which the terrifying splendour of the sacred idols might have removed it? Did it not drive out that superstition which suffocates imagination and faith by hewing down the sacred groves and pronouncing curses on the abominations of Moloch and Chemosh?

The fact that visual aids are employed for religious purposes has nothing to do with the dangers inherent in their untheological and irresponsible use. I venture to say that I have not yet seen a religious film (that is, a film of overtly religious intent) which did not frighten me with the thought of what that kind of thing may do to our religion. It is not easy to see why the film technique, with its abundant resources, has so signally failed to elevate the religious

[1] N. Micklem, *Religion Day by Day* (Independent Press, 1955), ch. 5.

mind when religious drama has in our generation produced such remarkable and inventive enrichments of our devotion as Charles Williams's *The Seed of Adam*, Anne Ridler's *The Trial of Thomas Cranmer*, Christopher Fry's *A Sleep of Prisoners*, and the work of R. H. Ward, not to mention the broadcast series *The Man Born to Be King*. But it is so,[1] and for the present I can only explain it by the fact that the directors of religious films have not yet mastered the techniques of artistic asceticism.

Two other things ought briefly to be said. One is that what St John of Damascus said about visual aids and their legitimacy, together with the Biblical warnings about them, must nowadays be applied equally to the use of the other arts in worship. The art of music has, of course, developed into self-consciousness long after the time of John of Damascus, let alone of the New Testament. The case for a technique of ascetism and discipline in its use has not yet been fully argued, and we will not go into it at all at this stage. Similarly architecture is undeniably a 'visual aid', and few Christians have openly denied that it is a legiti-

---

[1] It is only fair to give an example. I witnessed in the same year two films: one entitled *I Believe in You*, the other, *The Promise*. Both were made by the same well-known film organization. The first was for general release and the second for showing in churches. Curiously enough, both dealt with the experiences of probation officers. The first was exceedingly good entertainment, persuasive, serious in its intention, with plenty of humour and wit, and I dare to say fundamentally religious. The second, equally well acted and produced, was intended to be a story of conversion, and at its crucial point slipped into a sentimentality so disastrous that it was difficult to watch the remainder without embarrassment. It even ended with an awful hymn. I have no space to produce the detailed analysis of these reactions that I should be prepared to do another time; but the terrifying thing was to see the clear conviction in the producer's mind that humour and vitality and reality are 'life' and that sentimentality is 'religion'.

mate aid, although certain ages have produced architectural techniques that later ages have found difficult to associate with any recognizable religious sense. But again, we can leave this as a matter for further discussion.

The other thing to say is that the apparent iconoclasm of the Puritans (except, again, Cromwell's major-generals) is not so much an iconoclasm as the consequence of a feeling among them that they were in a special sense Men of the New Covenant, in a new way spiritually literate. The barrenness of the traditional meeting house (a thing of positive beauty contrasted with the pretentious adornments of the nineteenth-century nonconformist chapel) is really a gesture towards the simplicity that men who (however mistakenly) believe they have new insight into the Law of Christ feel they can afford to affect.

But the Church accepted images, and elected, as it always does, to live dangerously. Life would be easier if we all agreed that no art should be associated with worship. But it would be much less gracious. And the fact is that in one way and another all Christians use imagination and art in their presentation of the Faith. The question is, then, by what standards should it be laid under discipline and correction? Once again, we must urge that good doctrine will issue in good practice. A thoughtless condemnation of imagination will come from a false doctrine of man. A patronizing or a terrified attitude towards the material creation will come from a gnostical denial of the Incarnation. But more devastating than all these is the familiar modern dogma, which lays it down that the standard by which all art in church shall be judged shall be 'I like it' or 'I do not like it'; and that comes from a false doctrine of creation. For the ancient commandment said 'Thou shalt not bow down and worship' these things. To bow down and worship means to be enslaved to them. To say 'I like it' and 'I don't like it', and to use these phrases as a basis for action is to say, 'These things have power over me, and I cannot resist that power; so I must act as that power directs.' That is idolatry. That is the end of all vision. All the visual aids in the world, all the films and plays and architecture and music that the best artists can produce for us will not of themselves deliver us from that condemnation, 'Ye say, We see: therefore your sin remaineth.'

INDEX OF SUBJECTS AND NAMES

INDEX OF BIBLICAL REFERENCES